THE ART OF WILLIAM GOLDING

I am very serious. I believe that man suffers from an
appalling ignorance of his own nature. I produce my own view,
in the belief that it may be something like the truth.
I am fully engaged to the human dilemma but see it as far more
fundamental than a complex of taxes and astronomy.

—*William Golding*, in reply to a literary magazine's question-
naire, "The Writer in His Age"

BERNARD S. OLDSEY
& STANLEY WEINTRAUB

The Art of
William Golding

HARCOURT, BRACE & WORLD, INC., NEW YORK

C.11.68
Library of Congress Catalog Card Number: 65-23971
Printed in the United States of America

ACKNOWLEDGMENTS

The authors are indebted to *College English*, and James E. Miller,
Jr., its editor, for permission to use parts of their article "*Lord of
the Flies:* Beelzebub Revisited," which appeared in *College English*
in November, 1963.

For assistance and counsel they are further indebted to Charles
W. Mann, Henry W. Sams, and Frederick W. Matson, of the
Pennsylvania State University. An additional debt is owed collectively to the captive audience of Penn State's Comparative Literature Luncheon Club, which, at various times, swallowed parts of
four chapters of this volume after dessert, without any visible ill
effects.

They also wish to thank the following publishers for permission
to quote from the works cited: Coward-McCann, Inc., for *Lord of
the Flies* by William Golding, © 1954 by William Gerald Golding;
Harcourt, Brace & World, Inc., for William Golding's *Free Fall,
The Inheritors, Pincher Martin,* and *The Spire,* and for T. S.
Eliot's "Choruses from *The Rock*," "The Love Song of J. Alfred
Prufrock," "The Waste Land" (from *Collected Poems 1909–1962*),
and *The Rock;* Alfred A. Knopf, Inc., for *The Fall* by Albert
Camus, translated by Justin O'Brien.

For Ann & Rodelle

CONTENTS

1

WILLIAM GOLDING:
AN INTRODUCTION

How can one record and not invent?
Is there any point in understanding the nature
of a small boy crying?

—*William Golding, in "Billy the Kid"*

DEAN OF HIS generation of novelists, William Golding came to writing as his profession relatively late in life. Until his middle forties he was unknown, the postwar generation of English writers pouring out a decade's worth of angry and not-so-angry novels and plays while he—like many of the others, a demobilized veteran—earned his living as a provincial schoolmaster and experimented with fiction as an avocation.

A rather private man, Golding has permitted only brief glimpses into his life and background—the sort of thing provided in formal statements to *Who's Who*. The inevitable interviews to which he has submitted have added little to the biographical store; and only in his brief career as a book reviewer did he unbend freely and autobiographically—possibly one of the reasons he cut that career short. He has not been a publicized recluse, like J. D. Salinger, but he peers out at the world as through a bearded mask, and he has largely kept himself to himself except in his novels, which reveal the writer though perhaps not the man.

Golding was born on September 19, 1911, in Cornwall. It was some seven months before the *Titanic* went down, an event which may have—at second hand—provided him with some of the early impetus toward the philosophy which dominates his work, for he recalled his mother once confiding to him, when he was very young, that her awareness of the world as "an exhilarating but risky place" dated from the day on which she heard that the *Titanic* had sunk.[1] Later, in public school, he was reproved by a master for an offense clearly more horrendous to the offender than to the master; and he learned something more about the world to add to the developing rudiments of his philosophy. Begging for punishment, Golding was told, to his surprise, "You always want the easy way out." He was dismissed unpunished.[2]

Golding's childhood was a relatively isolated one. Of the time of his first day in school, he has written, "I had known no one outside my own family—nothing but walks with Lily [his nurse] or my parents, and long holidays by a Cornish sea. I had read much for my age but saw no point in figures. I had a passion for words in themselves, and collected them like stamps or birds' eggs. I had also a clear picture of what school was to bring me. It was to bring me fights. I lacked opposition,

[1] "Before the Beginning," a review of *World Prehistory* by Grahame Clark, *The Spectator*, May 26, 1961, p. 768.
[2] National Council of Teachers of English luncheon address by William Golding, San Francisco, November 30, 1963.

and yearned to be victorious. Achilles, Lancelot and Aeneas should have given me a sense of human nobility, but they gave me instead a desire to be a successful bruiser." [3]

Golding's Sammy Mountjoy (*Free Fall*), his head filled with tantalizing images, draws them in school copybooks meant for more legitimate uses. The young schoolboy William Gerald Golding, his head filled with images struggling to shape themselves, verbalized them in his own small breaches of discipline:

It did not occur to me that school might have discipline or that numbers might be necessary. While, therefore, I was supposed to be writing out my tables, or even dividing four oranges between two poor boys, I was more likely to be scrawling a list of words, butt (barrel), butter, butt (see goat). While I was supposed to be learning my Collect, I was likely to be chanting inside my head a list of delightful words which I had picked up God knows where—deebriss and Skirmishar, creskent and sweeside. On this first day, when Miss taxed me with my apparent inactivity, I smiled and said nothing, but nothing, until she went away.

. . . I looked at books or pictures, and made up words, dong-bulla for a carthorse; drew ships, and aeroplanes with all their strings, and waited for the bell. [4]

This passion for literature—and "for words in themselves"—lasted into the Marlborough Grammar School, where Golding received his secondary education, and persisted through his holidays back at a Cornish seaside, a period quite obviously recalled in passages in some of his early novels, particularly *Pincher Martin* and *Lord of the Flies*. He developed a particular passion for Greek—and still lists his recreations in

[3] "Billy the Kid," *The Spectator*, November 25, 1960, p. 808.
[4] *Ibid.*

Who's Who as sailing and Greek. *The Odyssey* was a source of unusual joy:

> I seem to remember that the last ten lines of book nine . . . came to me . . . as a sheer gift. There were grains of sand on the page, I remember, and by my ear the bristles of marron grass shuddered and stirred their small funnels in the dry, white sand. With that sea beating on the beach, it was not difficult to lie back, repeat the ancient words and hear the familiar surge and thunder.[5]

Golding read the classics of adulthood and the classics of childhood almost simultaneously, and made as little of the former as there may have been in the latter; yet both left their mark upon his writing in almost equally profound fashion. "I personally am stunned," he later observed, "when I think of what a passionless pattern I made of it all. If we revisit our childhood's reading, we are likely to discover that we missed the satire of *Gulliver*, the evangelism of *Pilgrim's Progress*, and the loneliness of *Robinson Crusoe*." He read Henty, Ballantyne, and Burroughs as well, long before he realized that they "require an innocence of approach which, while it is natural enough in a child, would be a mark of puerility in an adult. . . ." Seeing them later from a larger view was to be of personal literary significance to him, but at the time the classics of childhood satisfied him as they were—and as he was: "They held me rapt. I dived with the Nautilus, was shot round the moon, crossed Darkest Africa in a balloon, descended to the centre of the earth, drifted in the South Atlantic, dying of thirst, and tasted—oh rapture! It always sent me indoors for a drink--the fresh waters of the Amazon." [6]

---

[5] "Surge and Thunder," a review of the Robert Fitzgerald translation of *The Odyssey*, *The Spectator*, September 14, 1962, p. 370.
[6] "Appointment by Gaslight," a review of a series of Jules Verne reprints, *The Spectator*, June 9, 1961, p. 841.

In addition, he learned about what was missing in many of the books of his childhood from the household servants, who read aloud their letters when he was still young enough to be permitted access to their bedrooms. Servant girls let him leaf through copies of such subliterary magazines as *Peg's Paper*. Experiences like these combined to bring him both a minimal knowledge of love and a realization of the substantial gap between literature and life. He discovered, among other literarily useful things, that the gap between truth and beauty was wider than Keats had indicated.[7]

When Golding was about twelve he solemnly began his first novel. It was to be in twelve volumes, and was to incorporate a history of the rise of the trade-union movement. He never forgot the first sentence of the opus: "I was born in the Duchy of Cornwall on the eleventh of October, 1792, of rich but honest parents." That sentence set a standard he could not maintain, he has admitted, and the novel cycle went no further.[8]

It was hardly surprising that Golding, son of a distinguished British schoolmaster, should have been devoted to literature early in life, and should have later become a schoolmaster himself. Still, the route he took between his own early schooling and his first career was a circuitous one, for he entered Brasenose College, Oxford, intending to major in science. More than two years passed before he decided that he had erred, and he switched to English literature. Even there his interests veered as far from modern science as was possible, in the direction of Anglo-Saxon language and literature. (He considers *The Battle of Maldon*, ca. tenth century, one of his chief literary influences, and its spirit may be seen in *The Inheritors*.) What

[7] National Council of Teachers of English luncheon address.
[8] *Ibid.*

have remained apparent in his writing are his academically split personality, his science-versus-the-humanities point of view, and his habit of running literary experiments which still smack of the laboratory he rejected.

After publishing a volume of poems in 1934,[9] he spent the rest of the thirties in relatively desultory fashion, venturing into writing, acting, and producing (much like his Christopher "Pincher" Martin) for a small non–West End London theater. (One of his roles was Danny, in the Emlyn Williams murder-thriller, *Night Must Fall*.) The drifting ended in 1939 when he married and accepted a teaching appointment at Bishop Words-worth's School in Salisbury; but he soon took leave from teaching and joined the Royal Navy. World War II had begun, and Golding was to spend nearly the entire war in naval service. His last assignment was as a lieutenant in command of a rocket-firing ship, after he had seen action against German warships, and in antisubmarine and antiaircraft operations, and had participated in D-day naval support of the landing in France. Once, coming close to the experience of one of his fictional creations, he was adrift for three days in the English Channel. He acquired, according to his account, an unwarranted reputation for loving tense combat situations, because "at moments of stress in the middle of action, his facial muscles would contract violently, producing a broad ghastly grin, which was interpreted by his men as pure delight of combat." [10] A more accurate

[9] Golding has told an interviewer, "I don't own a copy. But I suppose there's one somewhere. Yes, at the British Museum. The Bodleian [too], of course. Actually, I'd rather forget it. . . . You might say I write prose because I can't write poetry." Bernard F. Dick, " 'The Novelist Is a Displaced Person': An Interview with William Golding," *College English*, XXVI (March, 1965), 480.
[10] E. L. Epstein, "Notes on William Golding and *Pincher Martin*," an appendix to the Capricorn edition of *Pincher Martin*, p. 212.

understanding of Golding during the war years could have been arrived at through observation of the consolation he found in reading and rereading Homer, rediscovering through the epics a sense of the continuity of human history.

When the war ended in 1945, Golding returned to Bishop Wordsworth's School to teach, with new insights, English and philosophy. He also began to write, producing, among other things, the "rubbish" of parodies and parallels to other writers' styles (which may have been subtly influential in his later development of a literary method), as well as four novels no publisher would accept. Later, he mused wryly over the way he refused to accept his unsalability, and kept writing:

When I have tried every publisher there is and still have been turned down, and am still haunted by this desperate, cruel, bloody business of believing I can write—when all the ways are blocked, I can think of one left. I shall take my MSS aboard a boat. I shall go to Egypt. I shall get up the Nile to Oxyrhynchus, walk into the dumb, dry desert and bury the lot next to the city rubbish tip. In 5000 AD they will be excavated by Pekin University, and published among the seven hundred and fifty volumes of *Vestiges of Western Literature*. Of course no one will read them, any more than they read Erinna or Bacchylides. This obsession with writing is pointless as alcoholism and there's no Authors Anonymous to wean you from the typewriter.[11]

In 1954 *Lord of the Flies* became the first of Golding's novels to be published, but enthusiasm for it (as well as for the novels which followed close upon it) was relatively slow in developing, although the initial critical reception was good. *The Inheritors* was published in 1955 (in the United States it

[11] "It's a Long Way to Oxyrhynchus," *The Spectator*, July 7, 1961, p. 9.

was not published until 1963), *Pincher Martin* in 1956, and *Free Fall* in 1959. By 1959 Golding's novels were appearing in paperback editions, and reaching a wide audience (particularly in universities), and were becoming the subject of critical controversies in popular and scholarly publications. Both events were signs of a variety of success which had been long in coming. In 1961 he retired from his teaching post in Salisbury to devote more time to writing.

After a decade of Golding's public exposure as a novelist, critical attitudes toward him had coalesced into, on the one hand, a scholarly, often pedantic, skepticism; and, on the other, a feeling that "No English novelist of his generation has dared —and achieved—as much." [12] Certainly few novels which demanded so much from their readers remained as long on the best-seller lists in Great Britain and the United States as did Golding's *The Spire* in 1964, nor did any such work have so divided a critical reception. The school of skepticism (based on a certain amount of emotional hostility to Golding's unchanging point of view) acquired, between *Lord of the Flies* and *The Spire*, a number of its later converts from among the band of early Golding followers. Some altered their positions on literary grounds, some on philosophical grounds ("Better to get back to humanism . . ." V. S. Pritchett commented in 1964). The shift in attitudes represents what is almost a cliché in the history of literary criticism. "A great man," Sir Max Beerbohm once observed, "cannot be appreciated fully by his intimate contemporaries. Nor can his success be ever quite palatable to them, however actively they may have striven to win it for him. To fight for a prince who has to be hiding in

[12] David Lodge, "William Golding," *The Spectator,* April 10, 1964, p. 489.

an oak-tree is a gallant and pleasant adventure; but when one sees the poor creature enthroned, with a crown on his head and a sceptre in his hand, one's sentiments are apt to cool. . . . The old torches are still waved, but perfunctorily; and the main energy is devoted to throwing cold water." [13]

Golding's actual position in his generation is almost unique. There is no easy way to fit him into any current English school of fiction. Nevertheless, his novels, Walter Allen notes, "strike one as strictly contemporary; they are rooted in the anguish and anxiety of their times." [14] Paradoxically, this is so even though only one (*Free Fall*) of the first half-dozen major works he has published is set in a conventional contemporary environment. The novels of isolation, *Lord of the Flies* and *Pincher Martin*, are almost outside time. Each of Golding's novels is a remarkable imaginative feat, fertile in invention, powerful in drama, suggestive in its richness of literary and mythic overtones. By comparison the symbolic novels of Iris Murdoch become emptily brilliant, the comic grotesques of Kingsley Amis thin, the detail-laden satire of Angus Wilson without depth, the social realism of John Braine pallid, the exotic sensuality of Lawrence Durrell too easily florid, the socio-psychology of C. P. Snow's novel cycle ponderous and stolid. *Sui generis*, he is not any more likely to follow any school than he is to found one; yet he has become one of the most significant novelists writing in English, and—an irony, considering the intellectual demands he places upon his readers—one of the most read.

[13] "Mr. Shaw's Position," in *Around Theatres* (New York, 1954), pp. 412–13.
[14] *The Modern Novel* (New York, 1964), p. 288.

An examination of his fictional perspectives, and of how his view of the world is worked out in his writings, seems from these standpoints to be a useful objective. This volume is an attempt to point out one of the directions such an examination should take.

2

BEELZEBUB REVISITED:
LORD OF THE FLIES

"I am by nature an optimist; but a defective logic—
or a logic which I sometimes hope desperately
is defective—makes a pessimist of me."

—*William Golding, "On the Crest of the Wave"*

*L*ord of the Flies (1954), Golding's first novel and the one that established his reputation, is still most widely acclaimed as his major work. Not only has it captured a large segment of the popular and academic imagination (having the effect there of replacing J. D. Salinger's *The Catcher in the Rye*), but it has also attracted the greatest amount of critical attention directed toward Golding.

To date, that critical attention has proven various, specialized, and spotty. A remarkable "first novel" on any terms, *Lord of the Flies* has been praised on literary grounds much less often than as sociological, psychological, or religious tract, as "pure parable," fable, or myth.[1] The terminology of Frazer and Freud are more often brought to bear upon the novel than the yardsticks of literary criticism. As literature, however, it has been—even while praised—called unoriginal and derivative, filled with "gimmickry," devoid of characterization, and lacking in logic.[2] Only twice has it been blasted as insignificant art encased in bad writing.[3]

Certainly *Lord of the Flies* is derivative, in the sense that it falls well within the main stream of several English literary traditions. It is a "boys' book," as are *Treasure Island, The Wind in the Willows, High Wind in Jamaica,* and other books primarily about juvenile characters which transcend juvenile appeal; it is in the tradition of the survival narrative, along with *Robinson Crusoe, The Swiss Family Robinson,* and even

[1] See, for example, John Peter, "The Fables of William Golding," *Kenyon Review,* XIX (Fall, 1957), 577–92; Claire Rosenfield, "'Men of Smaller Growth': A Psychological Analysis of William Golding's *Lord of the Flies,*" *Literature and Psychology,* XI (Autumn, 1961), 93–101; and Edmund Fuller, "The Compelling Lure of William Golding," *New York Herald Tribune Books,* November 4, 1962, pp. 1, 3.

[2] Carl Niemeyer, in "The Coral Island Revisited," *College English,* XXII (January, 1961), 241–45, makes explicit Golding's use of R. M. Ballantyne's *The Coral Island,* a boys' book published in 1857; and James Gindin, in "'Gimmick' and Metaphor in the Novels of William Golding," *Modern Fiction Studies,* VI (Summer, 1960), 145–52, tries to indicate how much of Golding's work is marred by "clever tricks."

[3] There is some adverse criticism of Golding, on the grounds of "gimmick" or philosophy, but Martin Green's "Distaste for the Contemporary," *The Nation,* May 21, 1960, pp. 451–54, seems egregiously harsh and willful, and R. C. Townsend's "Lord of the Flies: Fool's Gold?," *Journal of General Education,* XVI (July, 1964), 153–60, is a specious denigration of *Lord of the Flies* through a working out of proposed parallels with *A High Wind in Jamaica,* Golding coming off second best philosophically and stylistically each time. Kenneth Rexroth ("William Golding," *The Atlantic,* 215 [May, 1965], 96–98), like the French translator of *Lord of the Flies,* shows his failure to comprehend the book in his calling it merely a "carelessly documented" *Swiss Family Robinson.* All Golding's novels are "rigged," he adds.

Barrie's *Admirable Crichton;* it is in the tradition—best exemplified by Conrad, Cary, and Greene in our century—that examines our culture by transplanting it harshly to an exotic locale where it prospers or withers depending upon its intrinsic value and strength; it is in the long tradition of anti-science writing in England, where authors for centuries have equated scientific progress with dehumanization; and it at least appears to be in the Nonconformist English religious tradition, which assumes mankind's fall from grace.

If all these traditions lead back to one key source of inspiration, it may be no accident. The traditions embodied in *Lord of the Flies* can be discovered in *Gulliver's Travels*—Swift's version of the primeval savagery and greed which civilization only masks in modern man. It seems no coincidence that we also find in Golding a Swiftian obsession with physical ugliness, meanness, and nastiness (sometimes bordering on the scatological), and with the sense of how tenuous is the hold of intelligence, reason, and humaneness as a brake upon man's regression into barbarism.

Eventually, of course, Golding must be judged according to his individual talent rather than tradition or polemical appeal. Other critical visits to his minor devil's island have been accomplished mainly at a distance, through special field glasses. Here we revisit the island armed only with the knowledge that Golding is essentially a literary man who uses scene, character, and symbol (not to mention an exceedingly fine style and some admittedly tricky plot methods) to achieve imaginative literary effects.

The scenic qualities of *Lord of the Flies* help make it an imaginative work for the reader as well as the author. Although Golding occasionally provides consolidating detail, he more commonly requires the reader to pull narrative and descriptive elements into focus. For example, he provides no end-paper map or block description of his fictional island. The reader must explore it along with the participants in the story and piece together a usable concept of time and place. What we learn in this way is just enough to keep the work within the realm of fiction, but not enough to remove it from the realm of allegory. *And the essence of Golding's art resides exactly within the area of overlap.*

Fable-like, time and place are vague. The Queen (Elizabeth?) still reigns, and "Reds" are apparently the vague enemy. It is the postcatastrophic near-future, in which nuclear war has laid waste much of the West. ("They're all dead," Piggy thinks. And "civilization," corroborates Golding, is "in ruins.") The fiery crash of the boys' plane upon a tropical island has been the final stage of their evacuation from England. The island seems to lie somewhere in the Indian or Pacific Ocean, probably on a line extending from England to Australia, which could well have been the planned terminus of their evacuation. Jack provides the clue for such geographical extrapolation when he speaks of Simon's seizures at "Gib." (Gibraltar) and "Addis" (Addis Ababa), as well as "at matins over the precentor." [4]

Shaped roughly like an outrigged boat, the boys' haven is a tropical island with a coral base. A mile out along one side runs a barrier reef, between which and the island lies a lagoon, on whose inward shore the boys hold their assemblies. At one end of the island there appears to be another, smaller island; but upon close inspection this is found to be attached by a rocky isthmus. Topographically, the island rises from low

[4] *Lord of the Flies* (New York: Capricorn Books, 1959). All subsequent references to the novel are to this edition.

jungle and orchard land to a mountaintop, or ridge, with few or no trees. By way of food, it provides the boys with bananas, coconuts, an "olive-grey, jelly-like fruit," and wild pig, as well as crab and fish taken from the sea. At midday the island gets hot enough to produce mirage effects.

If there were an end-paper map for Golding's island, it would no doubt be marked to indicate these major points of interest: (1) the beach along the lagoon, where Piggy and Ralph find the conch, and where assemblies are held near a natural platform of fallen trees; (2) the mountaintop, from which the island is surveyed, where the signal fire is placed, and where eventually the dead parachutist is trapped by wind and rock; (3) the burned-out quarter mile, where the mulberry-faced boy dies in the first fire; (4) Simon's leafy bower, to which he makes mystic retreats and from which he views the ceremony of impaling the pig's head upon a stake; (5) the orchard, where the fruit is picked and where some of the "littluns" are "taken short," leaving behind their fecal trail; (6) the "castle" at the tail end of the island, rising a hundred feet from the sea, where the first search for the "beast" is made, and where Piggy is killed after Jack has made this bastion his headquarters; and (7) the jungle, with its hanging vines that recall snakes and "beasties," with its pig trails where Jack hunts and where Ralph is finally hunted.

When the details are extracted and given order under an analytical light, Golding's island looks naturalistic in specification. But matters are not at all that clear in the book. The location of the island, for example, is kept deliberately vague: it is sufficiently remote to draw only two ships in a month or so, yet close enough to "civilization" to be the floor above which deadly, and old-fashioned, air battles are fought miles high (the boys' plane itself has been shot down). The nearby air and naval war in progress, with conventional weapons, is somewhat out of keeping with earlier reports of utter catastrophe. Equally incongruous is the smartly attired naval officer and savior of the closing pages, whose jaunty mien is incompatible with catastrophe. Yet he is as important to the machinery of the allegory as the earlier crash, which is equally difficult to explain on rational grounds. During the crash the fuselage of the evacuation plane has apparently broken in two: the forward half (holding pilot and others, including more boys) has been cleanly washed out to sea by a conveniently concomitant storm; and the after-section (which makes a long fiery scar as it cuts through the jungle) tumbles unscathed children onto the island. As incompatible, obscure, askew, and unrealistic as these elements may be, they are no more so than Gulliver's adventures. And Golding's graphically novelistic character and topographic details, both poetic and naturalistic, tend to blur the fabulous qualities of the narrative's use of time and setting in its opening and close. Although it is enough to say that the fabulist must be permitted pegs upon which to hang his fable, it is Golding's richly novelistic elements of the telling that call attention to the subtle dissonance. Paradoxically—yet artistically—this very tension between realistic novel and allegorical fable imparts to *Lord of the Flies* some of its unique power.

Golding's characters, like his setting, represent neither fictional reality nor fabulistic unreality, but, rather, partake of the naturalistic and the allegorical at the same time. As a result, they emerge more full bodied than Kafka's ethereal forms, more subtly shaded than Orwell's animal-farm types, and more comprehensibly motivated than Bunyan's religious ciphers. Bit by bit we can piece together fairly solid pictures of the major figures in *Lord of the Flies*. And since a number of commentators have fallen into interpretative error by precipitously trying to state what these characters "mean," perhaps it would be best here to start by trying to state what they "are."

Ralph, the protagonist, is a boy twelve years and a "few months" old. He enters naïvely, turning handsprings of joy upon finding himself in an exciting place free of adult supervision. But his role turns responsible as leadership is thrust upon him—partly because of his size, partly because of his attractive appearance, and partly because of the conch with which, like some miniature Roland, he has blown the first assembly. Ralph is probably the largest boy on the island (built like a boxer, he nevertheless has a "mildness about his mouth and eyes that proclaimed no devil"). But he is not so intellectual and logical as Piggy ("he would never be a very good chess player," Golding assures us), not so intuitively right as Simon, nor even so aggressively able to take advantage of opportunity as Jack. For these reasons there has been some reader tendency to play down Ralph as a rather befuddled Everyman, a straw boy of democracy tossed about by forces he cannot cope with. Yet he should emerge from this rites-of-passage *bildungsroman* with the reader's respect. He is as much a hero as we are allowed: he has courage, he has good intelligence, he is diplomatic (in assuaging Piggy's feelings and dividing authority with Jack), and he elicits perhaps our greatest sympathy (when hounded across the island). Although he tries to live by the rules, Ralph is no monster of goodness. He himself becomes disillusioned with democratic procedure; he unthinkingly gives away Piggy's embarrassing nickname; and, much more importantly, he takes part in Simon's murder! But the true measure of Ralph's character is that he despairs of democracy because of its hollowness ("talk, talk, talk"), and that he apologizes to Piggy for the minor betrayal, and that—while Piggy tries to escape his share of the guilt for Simon's death—Ralph cannot be the hypocrite (this reversal, incidentally, spoils the picture often given of Piggy as superego or conscience). Ralph accepts his share of guilt in the mass action against Simon, just as he accepts leadership and dedication to the idea of seeking rescue. He too, as he confesses, would like to go hunting and swimming, but he builds shelters, tries to keep the island clean (thus combating the flies), and concentrates vainly on keeping a signal fire going. At the novel's end Ralph has emerged from his age of innocence; he sheds tears of experience, after having proven himself a "man" of humanistic faith and action. We can admire his insistence upon individual responsibility—a major Golding preoccupation—upon doing what must be done rather than what one would rather do.

Ralph's antagonist, Jack (the choir leader who becomes the text's Esau), is approximately the same age. He is a tall, thin, bony boy with light blue eyes and indicative red hair; he is quick to anger, prideful, aggressive, physically tough, and courageous. But although he shows traces of the demagogue from the beginning, he must undergo a metamorphosis from a timidity-shielding arrogance to conscienceless cruelty. At first he is even less able to wound a pig than is Ralph, but he is altered much in the manner of the transformation of the twentieth-century dictator from his first tentative stirrings of power lust to eventual bestiality. Although Golding is careful to show little of the devil in Ralph, he nicely depicts Jack as being directly in league with the lord of flies and dung.[5] Jack trails the pigs by their olive-green, smooth, and steaming

---

[5] The Lord of the Flies is not only Beelzebub and the endless variations upon him, but, in Greco-Roman tradition, the all-mighty Zeus, described (for example, in Sartre's play *The Flies*) as "god of flies and death. The

droppings. In one place we are shown him deep in animalistic regression, casting this way and that until he finds what he wants: "The ground was turned over near the pig-run and there were droppings that steamed. Jack bent down to them as though he loved them." His fate determined, Jack is a compelled being; he is swallowed by the beast—as it were—even before Simon: "He tried to convey the compulsion to track down and kill that was swallowing him up." Jack's Faustian reward is power through perception. He perceives almost intuitively the use of mask, dance, ritual, and propitiation to ward off—and yet encourage simultaneously—fear of the unknown. Propitiation is a recognition not only of the need to pacify but also of something to be pacified. In this instance it is the recognition of evil. "The devil must have his due," we say. Here the "beast" must be mollified, given its due. Jack recognizes this fact, even if he and his group of hunters do not understand it. Politically and anthropologically he is more instinctive than Ralph. Jack does not symbolize chaos, as sometimes claimed, but, rather, a stronger, more primitive order than Ralph provides.

Jack's chief henchman, Roger, is not so subtly or complexly characterized, and seems to belong more to Orwellian political fable. Slightly younger and physically weaker, he possesses from the beginning all the sadistic attributes of the demagogue's

---

image has white eyes and blood-smeared cheeks." To the naïve Orestes, Sartre's Zeus explains that the carrion-attracted flies are "a symbol," representative of a need in "all those creeping, half-human creatures" called men: "They have guilty consciences, they're afraid—and fear and guilty consciences have a good savor in the nostrils of the gods. Yes, the gods take pleasure in such poor souls. . . . What, moreover, could you give them in exchange? Good digestions, the gray monotony of provincial life, and the boredom—ah, the soul-destroying boredom—of long days of mild content. Go your way, my lad, go your way. The repose of cities and men's souls hangs on a thread. . . ."

hangman underling. In his treatment of the sow he proves deserving of his appellation in English slang. Through his intense, furtive, silent qualities, he acts as a sinister foil to Simon. By the end of the novel Golding has revealed Roger; we hardly need to be told that "the hangman's horror clung round him."

Simon is perhaps the most effectively—and certainly the most poignantly—characterized of all. A "skinny, vivid little boy, with a glance coming up from under a hut of straight hair that hung down, black and coarse," he is (at nine or ten) the lonely visionary, the clear-sighted realist, logical,[6] sensitive, and mature beyond his years. We learn that he has a history of epileptic seizures—a dubious endowment sometimes credited to great men of the past, particularly those with a touch of the mystic. We see the unusual grace and sensitivity of his personality crop up here and there as the story unfolds until he becomes the central figure of the "Lord of the Flies" scene— one of Golding's most powerful and poetic. We see Simon's instinctive compassion and intelligence as he approaches the rotting corpse of the parachutist, which, imprisoned in the rocks on the hill in flying suit and parachute harness, is the only palpable "monster" on the island. Although Simon's senses force him to vomit with revulsion, he nevertheless frees it "from the wind's indignity." When he returns to tell his frightened, blood-crazed companions that, in effect, they have nothing to fear but fear itself, his murder becomes the martyrdom of a saint and prophet, a point in human degeneration next to which the wanton killing of Piggy is but an anticlimax. In some of the novel's richest, most sensitive prose, the body

[6] Simon is usually thought of as being mystical or prophetic, but he is also as logical as any of the others, even Piggy.

of Simon (the boys' "beast" from the jungle) is taken out to sea by the tide, Golding here reaching close to tragic exaltation as Simon is literally transfigured in death: [7]

. . . The beast lay huddled on the pale beach and the stains spread, inch by inch.

The edge of the lagoon became a streak of phosphorescence which advanced minutely, as the great wave of the tide flowed. The clear water mirrored the clear sky and the angular bright constellations. The line of phosphorescence bulged about the sand grains and little pebbles; it held them each in a dimple of tension, then suddenly accepted them with an inaudible syllable and moved on.

Along the shoreward edge of the shallows the advancing clearness was full of strange, moonbeam-bodied creatures with fiery eyes. Here and there a larger pebble clung to its own air and was covered with a coat of pearls. The tide swelled in over the rain-pitted sand and smoothed everything with a layer of silver. Now it touched the first of the stains that seeped from the broken body and the creatures made a moving patch of light as they gathered at the edge. The water rose farther and dressed Simon's coarse hair with brightness. The line of his cheek silvered and the turn of his shoulder became sculptured marble. The strange attendant creatures, with their fiery eyes and trailing vapors, busied themselves round his head. The body lifted a fraction of an inch from the sand and a bubble of air escaped from the mouth with a wet plop. Then it turned gently in the water.

---

[7] Any attack that concentrates on Golding's style should come to grips with the kind of writing used to depict this scene. Martin Green's article does not. Nor does Kenneth Rexroth's attempt at deflation (*The Atlantic*, *op. cit.*). Golding not only writes about Neanderthals, according to Rexroth, "he writes for them. His message is not unlike that of Jack London. . . . Golding's prose is almost as bad. In some ways it is worse, because it lacks specificity. In London there is a degree of sensual immediacy and passionate rhetoric unknown to Golding." Clearly, Rexroth has scanned Golding rather cursorily.

Somewhere over the darkened curve of the world the sun and moon were pulling, and the film of water on the earth planet was held, bulging slightly on one side while the solid core turned. The great wave of the tide moved farther along the island and the water lifted. Softly, surrounded by a fringe of inquisitive bright creatures, itself a silver shape beneath the steadfast constellations, Simon's dead body moved out toward the open sea.

With his mysterious touch of greatness Simon comes closest to foreshadowing the kind of hero Golding himself has seen as representing man's greatest need if he is to advance in his humanity—the Saint Augustines, Shakespeares, and Mozarts, "inexplicable, miraculous." [8] Piggy, on the other hand, who, just before his own violent death, clutches at a rationalization for Simon's murder, has all the good and bad attributes of the weaker sort of intellectual. Despised by Jack and protected by Ralph, he is set off from the others by his spectacles, asthma, accent, and very fat, short body. Freudian analysts would have Piggy stand as superego, but he is extremely id-directed toward food: it is Ralph who must try to hold him back from accepting Jack's pig meat, and Ralph who acts as strong conscience in making Piggy accept partial responsibility for Simon's death. [9] Although ranked as one of the "biguns," Piggy is physically incapable and emotionally immature. The logic of his mind is insufficient to cope with the human problems of their coral-island situation. But this insight into him is fictionally denied to the Ralphs of this world, who (as on the last page of the novel) weep not for Simon, but for "the true, wise friend called Piggy."

How many children originally landed on the island alive

[8] William Golding, "On the Crest of the Wave," *The Writer's Dilemma* (London, 1961), pp. 42-51.
[9] Psychoanalytical articles thus far published fail to account for such behavior.

we never learn; however, we do know that there were more than the eighteen boys whose names are actually mentioned in the course of the novel. Census matters are not helped by the first signal fire, for it goes out of control and scatters the boys in fright. Ralph, worried about the littluns, accuses Piggy of dereliction of duty in not making a list of names. Piggy is exaggeratedly indignant: "How could I . . . all by myself? They waited for two minutes, then they fell in the sea; they went into the forest; they just scattered everywhere. How was I to know which was which?" But only one child known to any of the survivors has clearly disappeared—a small unnamed boy with a mulberry-marked face. This fact lends little credence to Piggy's tale of decimation.

Of those who remain, at least a dozen of whom are littluns, a significant number come alive through Golding's ability to characterize memorably with a few deft lines. Only two have surnames as well as Christian names: Jack Merridew, already mentioned as Ralph's rival, and the littlun Percival Wemys Madison. Jack at first demands to be called, as at school, "Merridew," the surname his mark of superior age and authority. Percival Wemys Madison ("The Vicarage, Harcourt St. Anthony, Hants, telephone, telephone, tele—") clutches vainly at the civilized incantation, learned by rote—in case he should get lost. And he is. His distant past has so completely receded by the end of the novel that he can get no farther in self-identification than "I'm, I'm—" for he "sought in his head for an incantation that had faded clean away." We learn little more about him, and hardly need to. Here again, in characterization, Golding's straddling the boundary line between allegory and naturalism demonstrates either the paradoxical power of his weakness as novelist or his ability to make the most of his shortcomings.

Whatever the case, Percival Wemys Madison epitomizes

the novel and underlines its theme, in his regression to the point of reduced existence. In fact, most of Golding's characters suggest more than themselves, contributing to critical controversy as well as the total significance of the novel. In the years of exegesis since publication of *Lord of the Flies*, critical analysis has been hardening into dogmatic opinion, much of it allegoristic, as evidenced by such titles as "Allegories of Innocence," "Secret Parables," and "The Fables of William Golding." [10] And even where the titles are not indicative (as with E. L. Epstein's Capricorn edition afterword, and the equally Freudian analysis of Claire Rosenfield),[11] critical literature has generally forced the book into a neat allegorical novel. The temptation is strong, since the novel is evocative and the characters seem to beg for placement within handy categories of meaning—political, sociological, religious, and psychological categories. Yet Golding is a simply complicated writer; and, so much the better for the novel as novel, none of the boxes fits precisely.

Oversimplifying, Frederick Karl writes that "When the boys

---

[10] John Peter's perceptive article has already been noted; see also Millar Maclure, "Allegories of Innocence," *Dalhousie Review*, XL (Summer, 1960), 145–56; and V. S. Pritchett, "Secret Parables," *New Statesman*, August 2, 1958, p. 146.

[11] Both Epstein and Rosenfield concentrate on the Freudian concept of id, ego, superego; but Epstein makes his most original analytical point with the Oedipal wedding night aspect of the sow's death. Golding has commented to an interviewer: "Yes, what is all this talk about Oedipal wedding nights, ids and egos? *And to think I've never read Freud in my life.* Someone wrote a terribly erudite article showing that Ralph was an id and Piggy an ego. Or was it the other way around? I was quite impressed, but the whole thing was simply untrue. I suppose I'm doing the same thing as Freud did—investigating this complex phenomenon called man. Perhaps our results are similar, but there is no influence." Bernard F. Dick, in "The Novelist Is a Displaced Person," *College English*, XXVI, 481.

on the island struggle for supremacy, they re-enact a ritual of the adult world, as much as the college Fellows in Snow's *The Masters* work out the ritual of a power struggle in the larger world." [12] Jack may appear to be the demagogic dictator and Roger his sadistic henchman; Ralph may be a confused democrat, with Piggy his "brain trust"; but the neatness of the political allegory is complicated by the clear importance of the mystical, generalization-defying Simon. Although Simon, who alone among the boys has gone up to the mountaintop and discovered the truth, is sacrificed in a subhuman orgy, those who have seen a religious allegory in the novel find it more in the fall of man from paradise, as the island Eden turns into a fiery hell, and the Satanic Jack into the fallen archangel. But Ralph makes only a tenuous Adam; the sow is a sorry Eve; and Piggy, the sightless sage, has no comfortable place in Christian myth. Further, it is an ironic commentary upon religious interpretations of *Lord of the Flies* that of an island full of choirboys, not one ever resorts—even automatically—to prayer or to appeals to a deity, not even before they begin backsliding. And the Edenic quality of the island paradise is compromised from the beginning, for, although the essentials of life are abundant, so are the essentials of pain, terror, and death: the fruit which makes them ill, the animals which awaken their bloodthirstiness and greed, the cruel war in the air above them, the darkness and the unknown which beget their fears.

As a social allegory of human regression the novel is more easily (perhaps too neatly) explainable as "the way in which, when the civilized restraints which we impose on ourselves are abandoned, the passions of anger, lust and fear wash across

[12] *The Contemporary English Novel* (New York, 1962), p. 258.

the mind, obliterating commonsense and care, and life once again becomes nasty, brutish and short." [13] The island itself is shaped like a boat, and takes on symbolic proportions, not simply in the microcosmic-macrocosmic sense, but as subtle foreshadowing of the regression about to take place among the boys: "It was roughly boat-shaped. . . . The tide was running so that long streaks of foam tailed away from the reef and for a moment they felt that the boat was moving steadily astern." This sternward movement not only conjures up the regressive backsliding away from civilization that constitutes the theme of the novel, but is imagistically associated with Piggy's "ass-mar" and the general note of scatology—as with the littluns being "taken short" in the orchard—which prevails in this book on Beelzebub, lord of the flies *and* dung. Later, when Simon asks the assembly to think of the dirtiest thing imaginable, Jack answers with the monosyllable for excrement. This is not what Simon means at all: he is thinking of the evil in man. But the two concepts merge in Golding's imagination— covertly in *Lord of the Flies* and manifestly in *Free Fall*, which is a literary cloaca, full of that revulsion psychologists try to explain in terms of the proximity and ambiguity of the apertures utilized for birth and excreta.

Some critics who see the allegory of evil as just the surface meaning of the novel have been led into psychological labyrinths, where Jack appears as the Freudian id personified; Ralph the ego; and Piggy the superego, conscience of the grown-up world. But William Wasserstrom has dealt severely with Miss Rosenfield in this kind of interpretation; the experts

[13] J. Bowen, "One Man's Meat: The Idea of Individual Responsibility in Golding's Fiction," London *Times Literary Supplement*, August 7, 1959, p. xii.

have fallen out;[14] and, besides, the Freudian *ménage à trois* fails to accommodate the vital Simon. Indeed, the problem in all attempts to explain *Lord of the Flies* as some kind of parable is that the novel is not a parable: it is too long, and lacks the point-by-point parallelism necessary to meet the definition. Nor, in the precise sense, is it a fable, since it deals primarily with human beings, since it does not rely upon folkloristic or fantastic materials, and since it does not provide the convenience of an explicit moral. It *is* allegoristic, rich in variant suggestions, and best taken at the level of suggestive analysis.

This novel has been taken, too, as a straight tale of initiation, with Ralph as hero—an interpretation to which the book's ending is particularly susceptible. Yet there is more to it than Ralph's facing a brutal adult world with a lament for his lost childhood and for the innocence he thinks has been stripped from him. What Ralph dimly fathoms, the naval-officer "rescuer" cannot possibly understand—that the world, in the words of Shaw's Saint Joan, is not yet ready to receive its saints, neither its Simons nor even its Piggys and Ralphs. Whether he means it or not Golding provides a hopeful note, for even at mankind's present stage of development Piggy and Ralph, the latter with shame, relapse only slightly toward the barbarism of their contemporaries (and that of the officer, who is engaged in a no less barbaric war "outside"); while Simon withstands the powerful regressive pressures completely. That these three represent three-quarters of the novel's major characters defeats any explanation of the novel in totally pessimistic terms.

---

[14] William Wasserstrom and Claire Rosenfield, "An Exchange of Opinion concerning William Golding's *Lord of the Flies,*" *Literature and Psychology,* XII (Winter, 1962), 2-3, 11-12.

Almost endlessly, the four major characters are thematically suggestive, and are usually identified in the book with certain imagery and talismanic objects: Jack with blood and dung, with the mask of primitive tribalism (imagistically he is in league with the Lord of the Flies); Piggy with pigs' meat (his physical sloth and appetite and eventual sacrifice), with his glasses, which represent intellect and science (though they could hardly coax the sun into making fire); Ralph with the conch and signal fire, with comeliness and the call to duty, with communal hope (all shattered when the conch dwindles in power and is finally shattered, and the signal fire dies out). Again, however, it may be Simon—not so thematically suggestive as the others—who provides the best clues to the un-Swiftian side of Golding's intentions, for we recall not only his mysticism, his intelligence, his fragility, but also his association with the bees and butterflies that hover sweetly and innocently (by comparison with the flies) about the island, and the tragic beauty of his transfiguration. Perhaps it is Simon who best suggests Golding's optimism in the face of his apparent allegory of regression. "The human spirit," writes Golding, "is wider and more complex than the whole of the physical evolutionary system. . . . We shall have . . . to conform more and more closely to categories or go under. But the change in politics, in religion, in art, in literature will come, because it *will* come; because the human spirit is limitless and inexhaustible." Just around the corner, he promises, are the Saint Augustines, Shakespeares, and Mozarts: "Perhaps they are growing up now." [15]

What can be said of *Lord of the Flies* eventually is that, in structure and narrative method, it is Golding's simplest novel.

[15] "On the Crest of the Wave," p. 51.

It lacks the ironic mystification of *The Inheritors*, which results from the necessity of working through primitive brains making simple and often erroneous "pictures" of situations. It escapes the often cryptic involvement, the sudden wrench of context, that come from the stream of consciousness and recall methods of *Pincher Martin* and *Free Fall*. But it is not an obvious novel, as sometimes claimed. It shares with his other books an ending technique that constitutes a reversal—a sudden shift of viewpoint. Here the timely arrival of the naval officer acts as no concession to readers demanding a happy ending. What we get instead of "gimmick" or conventional *deus ex machina* is a necessary change of focus: the boys, who have grown almost titanic in their struggle, are suddenly seen again as boys, some merely tots, dirty-nosed and bedraggled. And then a retrospective irony results, since the boys deserve to be thought of as titanic: if they have been fighting our battle, we realize—with both hope and dismay—that mankind is still in something of a prepuberty stage. Thus *Lord of the Flies* ends as no act of hope or charity or even contrition. It is an act of recognition. The tone is peculiarly calm: Golding keeps his distance from his materials; he does not interfere or preach; and the material is made to speak for itself through a simplicity of prose style and a naturalistic-allegorical form. The vision of Golding is through both ends of the telescope.

Kenneth Burke has said that any novel is but the expansion of a single sentence, perhaps simply the expansion of a single gesture. In the same way, criticism of any writer is but the expansion of a single sentence definition. We place the author within a *genus* and then describe the *differentia*. We may eventually conclude that his work is *sui generis*, but the defining method helps us to this conclusion. Much the same thing is true if we try to place him by tracing his origins and the influences exerted on his work; and any analysis or evaluation of Golding's fiction must revolve around the compound question of originality and derivation, for although Golding has been called the most original English novelist of the last twenty or thirty years, it is becoming increasingly clear that his originality in prose is much like that of T. S. Eliot's in verse. Golding, in fact, stands as a remarkable example of how the individual talent operates within a strong tradition. Tradition (the English novelistic tradition primarily, but with elements derived from American, French, and Classical sources) leaves its mark on his work, but his work leaves its individual mark, and sometimes excoriatingly, on tradition. What has become apparent is that Golding is a literary counterpuncher. Put another way, *he is a reactionary in the most basic sense of the word*. Reacting strongly to certain disagreeable aspects of life and literature as he sees them, he writes with a revolutionary heat that is contained rather than exploded within his compressed style. Restoration rather than preservation is his aim: he would restore concepts of Belief, Free Will, Individual Responsibility, Sin, Forgiveness (or Atonement, anyway), Vision, and Divine Grace. He would restore principles in an unprincipled world; he would restore belief to a world of willful unbelievers.

From the outset of his career, Golding received critical recognition on the basis of his providing something new, something original (most early commentators put it down to his renovation of parable and fable as literary modes of serious expression). One early reaction to his work was that here at last the Home Counties had succeeded in bringing forth a voice capable of contending with the universal wilderness and the everlasting whirlwind. It might not be the voice of a

Dostoevsky or Melville or Conrad or Camus, but certainly it was not the voice of still another angry young man. With each successive novel Golding seemed to be marking an end to all that—the novel of manners, the novel of social commentary—and thus to the great tradition as well. It was as though he were pointing at *Howards End* as a literary cul-de-sac.

Aside from his novels, which did their own attesting, Golding himself lent credence to the idea that he was indeed original, something of an experimenter in the making of modern myths.[16] In a Third Programme radio discussion, for example, he expressed a wish to make each book say something different, and in a different way each time:

It seems to me that there's really very little point in writing a novel unless you do something that either you suspected you couldn't do, or which you are pretty certain nobody else has tried before. I don't think there's any point in writing two books that are like each other. . . .

I see, or I bring myself to see, a certain set of circumstances in a particular way. If it is the way everybody else sees them, then there is no point in writing a book.[17]

This self-portrait of Golding as literary experimenter is fairly accurate, but it needs expansion. In this connection, we should remember that he spent his first years at Oxford as a student of science before he switched emphasis to English literature. And there remains in his literary efforts something of the scientific stance—that of a white-coated experimenter working in the isolation of a laboratory, isolating in turn his literary elements on islands, promontories, and rocks, in closets,

[16] See Frank Kermode's "The Novels of William Golding," *International Literary Annual*, III (1961), 13–14.
[17] As quoted by John Bowen, "Bending Over Backwards," *Times Literary Supplement*, October 23, 1959, p. 608.

asylums, and prison camps. But in doing his experiments Golding inevitably has a finger stuck in someone else's lab book, along with a marginal note indicating what is wrong or at least what remains to be done. If we were allowed to expand Golding's statement about himself, we would have to—on the basis of what proves to be his practice—add this presumptuous comment: "I often see what others have been getting at, and disagree strongly. So I conduct counter-experiments with results that state: 'Not that way, but this.' "

All Golding's novels, products of his peculiar literary temperament and habit, are reactive experiments. The wonder is how habitual a process this has been. Piecemeal, several critics have nicely documented certain influences or stimuli affecting his work. Yet important instances have been left undiscovered, overlooked, underestimated. What remains to be said is that this reactive method of composition has become the *modus operandi*. It provides a key as to what Golding has derived from others and what he has provided that is original. Yet Golding has insisted, "But one book never comes out of another, and *The Coral Island* is not *Lord of the Flies*." And, adamantly, that *"one work does not come from another unless it is still-born."* [18] Nevertheless, with Golding the process may be, if he has created counter-experiments which are original fiction, not stillbirth but birth.

The process begins with *Lord of the Flies*, and here the critical documentation has been fairly solid. In separate essays Frank Kermode and Carl Niemeyer make it quite apparent that a strong connection exists between Golding's novel and one published almost exactly a century earlier, R. M. Ballan-

[18] Dick, "The Novelist Is a Displaced Person," *College English*, XXVI, 481.

tyne's *The Coral Island* (1857).[19] Golding reworks Ballantyne's basic situation, setting, and narrative episodes. Like Ballantyne in each respect, he isolates a group of English boys on a coral island that seems an earthly paradise, with a plentitude of fruit and coconuts. He introduces pig killings, cannibalistic tendencies, and the question of ghosts. He names three of his major characters Jack, Ralph, and Piggy in honor of Ballantyne's Jack, Ralph, and Peterkin Gay (the last might just as well be called Piggy, because in one instance, when he is off hunting pigs, Jack alludes to him with the phrase "When Greek meets Greek," the implication being, of course, when pig meets pig).

If Golding works closely to Ballantyne's outline, it is mainly to show by contrast to his own findings how inane the nineteenth-century experiment in youthful isolation was. Eventually the contrast shows through strongly. While Ballantyne's characters, for instance, are stout English lads who overcome evil introduced into their worldly paradise by natives and pirates, Golding's characters find evil within themselves and almost go under, until finally extricated by a *deus ex machina*. The officer who is the long arm of that godly machine underscores the difference between Golding's novel and Ballantyne's when he says with Old Boy naïveté: "Jolly good show. Like the Coral Island." Ralph looks at the officer dumbly, uncomprehendingly, and his look measures the distance between generations as well as the distance between the fictional visions of 1857 and 1954.

Knowing about Ballantyne's contribution to *Lord of the Flies* makes for a fuller and richer reading of the novel than might otherwise be obtained. To see how hollow a reading can result when the necessary connection is not made, one need

[19] See Niemeyer, *op. cit.*, and Kermode, *op. cit.*

simply read the French version, in which the English naval officer is made to speak for the benefit of an uninitiated audience: "L'officier l'encouragea du menton. —Oui, je comprends. La belle aventure. Les Robinsons . . ." *The Swiss Family Robinson* (and even *Robinson Crusoe*, if it is intended in the pluralization) will not do. (See *Sa Majesté des Mouches*, translated by Lola Tranec, Gallimard, Paris, 1956.) In ironic contrast to *Lord of the Flies*, Golding has written of *The Swiss Family Robinson*, "This is how children live when they are happy. . . . The days are endless and time has no meaning. . . . In the text, as ever, the children take a child's place. There is simply no possibility of juvenile delinquency. The [parental] guiding hand is gentle but adamant. . . ." [20]

As Kermode perceptively declares, the related books of Ballantyne and Golding can be used as documents in the history of ideas, Ballantyne's contribution belonging "inseparably to the period when boys were sent out of Arnoldian schools certified free of Original Sin," [21] ready to keep the Empire shipshape. Golding writes with a vivid sense of paradox, with the eyes of someone who has seen the Empire crumble and witnessed twentieth-century manifestations of Original Sin.

Although it has gone unnoticed or unmentioned in comparisons of Golding and Ballantyne, both authors use similar conclusions involving the technical assistance of the *deus ex machina*. Jack, Ralph, and Peterkin are in the clutches of savages near the conclusion of *Coral Island*; they believe they will never more see home, and await death, only to find their bonds severed, and themselves set free. A "teacher," who stands in the place of the naval officer in *Lord of the Flies*, acquaints

---

[20] "Islands," review of reprint editions of *Swiss Family Robinson* and *Treasure Island, The Spectator*, June 10, 1960, p. 844.
[21] Kermode, *op. cit.*

them with the miraculous fact that their captor, chief Tararo, "has embraced the Christian religion." This is no less a miracle in its way than the appearance of the naval officer who arrives just in the nick of time to save Golding's Ralph. Religion also appears in *Lord of the Flies* in truncated form: as already mentioned, some of the boys are choir members, but no prayer is ever heard. Religion enters only by way of hindsight and moralistic impingement from the outside, as the reader considers a hidden theme. In *The Coral Island*, as we can see by the quite Christian ending, it plays a central, well-advertised part. Not only are Ballantyne's youths invincible Britons, as they often call themselves, but they have faith, in the usual sense of the word. The Ralph of that group could be speaking for them all when under difficult pressures he remembers his mother's parting homily: "Ralph, my dearest child, always remember in the hour of danger to look to your Lord and Saviour Jesus Christ. He alone is both able and willing to save your body and soul." This is exactly what Golding's children do not do. Golding made clear why in an interview in which he explained his approach to the efficacy of *Coral Island* morality:

What I'm saying to myself is "don't be such a fool, you remember when you were a boy, a small boy, how you lived on that island with Ralph and Jack and Peterkin." . . . I said to myself finally, "Now you are grown up, you are adult; it's taken you a long time to become adult, but now you've got there you can see that people are not like that." There savagery would not be found in natives on an island. As like as not they would find savages who were kindly and uncomplicated and that the devil would rise out of the intellectual complications of the three white men in the island itself.[22]

---

[22] As quoted in *William Golding*, by Samuel Hynes (New York, 1964), pp. 7–8.

Although Golding does not provide easy answers to all the questions he raises in *Lord of the Flies*, it is clear that his religious answer is not Ballantyne's. The real savior in *Lord of the Flies* is not the naval officer, but Simon—and his voice goes unheeded, as once again the crucifixion takes place, this time without redemption or resurrection.

3

EVOLUTION BY GOLDING:

THE INHERITORS

"I see as I saw. I move as I did in the world of . . .
the pictures of men. They despair. I hear groans . . .
well, they are the groans of the dead to me."

> —*Joseph Conrad and Ford Madox Hueffer,*
> THE INHERITORS

"But the grisly folk we cannot begin to understand.
We cannot conceive in our different minds the strange
ideas that chased one another through those queerly-
shaped brains."

> —*H. G. Wells, "The Grisly Folk"*

*T*he *Inheritors* follows *Lord of the Flies* by one year in publication and is closely connected with it in source and theme. Both are variations on the same theme, played over a sliding scale of evolutionary concept. Together, they mark the beginning and end of what might be called Golding's "primitive period." They complement each other enough to deserve special reading as companion pieces. In fact, it begins to appear as if *The Inheritors* were conceived out of an impulse left over from the composition of Golding's first fictional offspring. But Golding considers *The Inheritors* his favorite of his novels as well as his best.

Lord of the Flies, as already noted, drew almost all of its reactive energy from R. M. Ballantyne's nineteenth-century novel of Christian good cheer, *The Coral Island*. *The Inheritors*, though a reactive work too, is a somewhat different case of literary influence, having at least three discernible sources, including a novel of exactly the same title done in 1901 by Joseph Conrad and Ford Madox Hueffer (Ford), as well as a cluster of connected works done by H. G. Wells. Still, one of the sources is again *The Coral Island*.

Clearly Golding had boned up on Ballantyne either just before or during his work on *Lord of the Flies*, and it is doubtful that within the space of a single intervening year he forgot Ballantyne's scenes of tribal combat—tinged as they are with the bloody effects of infanticide and cannibalism.[1] Clumsy these scenes may be, but they are powerful and memorable, and their basic elements do appear in Golding's depiction of opposing tribes in *The Inheritors*. What may be even more important is that Ballantyne follows his bloody tribal episodes with others in which supposedly superior whites (pirates in this instance) behave with a savagery as appalling as that displayed by the native "blacks." The implied thesis that civilization does not necessarily guarantee civilized acts could hardly have been lost on Golding, who once confessed—in discussing how he came to write such a book as *Lord of the Flies*—that

---

[1] Ballantyne depicts a tribe of about forty warriors pursuing another smaller group composed of men, women, and children. The pursuit, in canoes, ends on the coral island shore; here a bloody battle is fought; women and children are searched out of the woods; and the warriors begin to broil one of the fifteen enemy "survivors." This is not the only horror viewed by Jack, Ralph, and Peterkin, who are hidden behind some overhanging rocks. But they take no action until the chief of the warriors plucks an infant from its mother's breast and throws the child into the sea.

his own twentieth-century vision had been seared by the acts of superior whites in places like Belsen and Hiroshima.

It is a thesis of this order, although less Christianly orthodox and more fictionally subtle, that unites Golding's first two novels. The theme which they share might be expressed in some such way as this: "Man's climb up the ladder of evolution may or may not be the same thing as a climb up the chain of being, but in either case the attempted rise can lead to a long, long, immemorably long fall." To see how this is so, it is necessary to see how in *The Inheritors* the tribes of Lok and Tuami replace (on a somewhat grown-up level) those of Ralph and Jack respectively. This time Golding seems to contradict the real conclusion of his first novel, since this time he allows the more "civilized" of the tribes to triumph and thus become inheritors of the earth. The contradiction is only seeming, however, for although Tuami's people are Homo sapiens and appear to represent a step forward in man's climb, they are eventually revealed as being more savage in their vicious, lusting nature than are Lok's sub-sapiens folk. Like the youthful members of Jack's band, Tuami's people represent the *descent* of man quite literally—not straightforwardly in the Darwinian sense, but in the Biblical sense of The Fall. Peculiarly enough, the boys slide backward, through their own bedevilment, toward perdition; and the Neanderthals of Lok's tribe hunch forward—given a push by early-day Homo sapiens—toward the same perdition. In terms of evolution, Golding's universe as revealed in these two novels allows for precious little slippage, in either direction. Retrogression (*Lord of the Flies*) and progression (*The Inheritors*) meet and lead to the same fall.

The Descent of Man and Man's Fall (that is to say, rationalism versus religion, the scientific view versus spiritual vision) constitute the opposing concepts of Golding's constant thematic structure. This is true in each of his literary situations as they exist between Piggy and Simon, in *Lord of the Flies;* Pincher Martin and his friend Nathaniel, in *Pincher Martin;* Dr. Halde and the latter-day Sammy Mountjoy, as well as Nick Shale and Miss Pringle, in *Free Fall;* Roger Mason and Dean Jocelin, in *The Spire;* and Phanocles and the Emperor, in *The Brass Butterfly* (although this last situation calls for careful discussion, since Golding here shows himself to be, if religious, extremely heterodox and humanistic).

This motif of opposing views of man proves especially strong, however, in *The Inheritors,* as Golding's deliberate choice of epigraph indicates:

. . . We know very little of the appearance of the Neanderthal man, but this . . . seems to suggest an extreme hairiness, an ugliness, or a repulsive strangeness in his appearance over and above his low forehead, his beetle brows, his ape neck, and his inferior stature. . . . Says Sir Harry Johnston, in a survey of the rise of modern man in his *Views and Reviews:* "The dim racial remembrance of such gorilla-like monsters, with cunning brains, shambling gait, hairy bodies, strong teeth, and possibly cannibalistic tendencies, may be the germ of the ogre in folklore. . . ."

The passage comes from H. G. Wells's *Outline of History.* As a descendant work of Darwin, Spencer, and the French Encyclopedists, it is the sort of thing which twenty-five years ago used to turn up with high frequency on those lists of the World's Ten Most Important Books or the Ten Most Important Books in My Life. And it became an important work in Golding's life also. The question is how important, or in what way important?

Casually read, the epigraph might suggest simply a dim starting point for *The Inheritors*—almost as beguilingly simple an entry as the allusion to *Coral Island* at the end of *Lord of the Flies*. Early in the game of close reading, however, two critics had the initial good sense to see how important a clue Golding's epigraph is. As John Peter said, "The very core of the book is ironic, for its purpose is to play off against our smug prejudices —like those of the epigraph—a representation of their grounds that is as humiliating as it is unexpected." [2] And as John Bowen, sensing once more the reactive force of Golding's fiction, declared: "Once again something has been stood on its head— after *Coral Island*, H. G. Wells' *Outline of History*." [3] Eventually Golding himself made matters explicit, and in so doing provided information of a literary, biographical, and perhaps even psychoanalytical nature:

Wells' *Outline* played a great part in my life because my father was a rationalist, and the *Outline* was something he took neat. It is the rationalist gospel *in excelsis*. . . . By and by it seemed to me not to be large enough . . . too neat and too slick. And when I re-read it as an adult I came across his picture of Neanderthal man, our immediate predecessors, as being these gross brutal creatures who were possibly the basis of the mythological bad man. . . . I thought to myself that this is just absurd. . . . [4]

The key phrases to hold onto here are "re-read it as an adult" and "came across his picture." When we remember how closely Golding worked with Ballantyne, it seems probable that he did more than reread the *Outline*; he may very well

[2] "The Fables of William Golding," *Kenyon Review*, XIX (Autumn, 1957), 585.
[3] "Bending Over Backwards," *Times Literary Supplement*, October 23, 1959, p. 608.
[4] As quoted by Frank Kermode in "The Novels of William Golding," *International Literary Annual*, III (1961), 19.

have kept it propped open before him as he worked on his own book—for certainly he used it, and not simply as a springboard or thesis-meant-for-antithesis, but as a source of information and narrative detail. Actually, Wells may have become a bit maligned in all this discussion. It is true he took the rationalistic, Darwinian view, following whatever offerings of paleontology and anthropology were open to him; but he was not so simple-minded as Golding and his commentators might have us believe.[5] And the thing to be remembered is that his view of Homo neanderthalensis—as well as the eventual clash with Homo sapiens—is utilized by Golding (with two or three crucial changes designed to gain sympathy for the underman). Then again, Golding may very well have used more of Wells than the epigraph or the pertinent section (Book II, Chapters VI to X) of the *Outline* might indicate. It would have been no difficult matter (a natural thing, at that) to pick out of the bookshelf a copy of *The Short Stories of H. G. Wells* (1929)

[5] In the *Outline* (p. 64) Wells saw weaknesses and gaps in the scientific approach and foresaw objections to it. In fact, while speaking of certain religious attitudes, he shows how well he understood exactly the kind of objection Golding was going to make in fictional form: "Many individuals dissent from the scientific opinion, because *they feel it is more seemly to suppose that man has fallen rather than risen. . . .* The task of the historian is to deal not with what is seemly but with what is true. No considerable Christian body, indeed, now insists upon the exact and literal acceptance of the Bible narrative; to that the freedoms of great poetry are very properly conceded; and so long as the biologist does not insist upon an animal origin for the soul of man there is really no dispute. . . . It is not fair, however, to proceed to an account of man's descent without this preliminary intimation. The writer tells what he believes to be the truth, and it is not for him to state arguments of opponents which do not appear to him to be valid and to which he could not do justice." (Italics added) Ironically, World War II made Wells even more pessimistic than any of his younger contemporaries, including Golding; in his very last book, *Mind at the End of Its Tether* (a booklet, actually, published in 1946), he declares flatly: "The end of everything we call life is close at hand and cannot be evaded." The atomic bomb had finished the *Outline*.

to see what he might have done in a fictional way with the Stone Age materials and man's descent. Summarizing certain elements in Wells's combined works should indicate to what extent Golding utilized them.

Pages 63 to 100 in the *Outline* [6] are the ones on which Golding must have concentrated (the epigraph comes from page 88; the picture of Neanderthal man he mentions appears on page 81). Throughout this section of his work Wells follows the lead of various biological scientists—including Darwin, Sir Harry Johnston, Sir Arthur Keith, and Worthington Smith—in tracing the development of man through the theoretical stages of ground ape, Homo neanderthalensis, and finally Homo sapiens. The crux of his presentation comes in the form of a clash between the Mousterians (Neanderthals) and the true men (Homo sapiens). The Mousterians are described as having extremely sloped brows, nasal indentations for a nose, and no true chin. Unlike true men, they lack canine teeth, and they can use their great toes nearly as well as their thumbs in grasping objects. They are hairy, stooped, and sometimes run on all fours. (Golding describes Lok's people as "smallish, and bowed.") Wells compares the Mousterians with a subgroup of their species known as the Proplipithecus, an interesting little manly ape "the size of a small cat." They abhor water, except to drink it; they find meat in a dead state and eat it when it is semiputrid. They travel in familial bands of no more than a half-dozen to a dozen members under the rule of "The Old Man." These people, according to Wells's account, seem to have buried their dead with respect and perhaps even ceremony.

In the later postglacial Paleolithic period an enormous leap

---

[6] The edition referred to is that of the Garden City Publishing Company (Garden City, New York, 1931).

forward is indicated by the appearance of the first true men, possessors of a hand and forebrain like our own. They dispossessed Homo neanderthalensis from his caverns and places by the rivers. They did not intermingle with the Neanderthals, looking down upon them as an entirely different species. These new men "drew on bones and antlers; they carved little figures." (Anyone who has read *The Inheritors* and wants to play literary detective can find plenty of clues in the drawings and figures reproduced on pages 89, 91, and 98 of the *Outline*. Items: ivory and bone knife points—of the sort Tuami makes at the novel's close; a large horned animal—of the kind Tuami draws on the ground; an antlered stag head done on ivory—like the totemic device of Marlan's tribe; and a small, rotund female figure ripened as though in pregnancy—resembling the Oa figure of Lok's tribe.) Besides their art, the new people have bows and arrows, spears, and pottery. And, having learned how to utilize bodies of water rather than fear them, they eventually become lake and river dwellers.

Wells felt great interest in the clash that anthropologists infer must have taken place between Mousterian men and the first true men. Condensing and reshaping materials used to describe man's descent in his *Outline*, he wrote a semidocumentary story called "The Grisly Folk." Done two years after the *Outline* was published, this is obviously an imaginative effort to fill out the expository account.

Wells informs his reader of primitive man through the testimony of inanimate objects and implements, tracing the stages of development through which man has passed. Typically, he begins "The Grisly Folk" with the words "Can these bones live?" And from there Wells begins to reconstruct his story from an archeological and anthropological viewpoint. He traces elements of primitive man's art, religion, and familial government. The approach is rational, denotative, and expository. Golding, on the other hand, hunches his way back to the past (though knowing something of what the books say about anthropology and paleontology) by utilizing what he knows of the present. Primitive man resides within us as children and adults just as plainly as the coccyx remains a vestige of an earlier form of human life. The point for Golding is that primitive man is in a way still our contemporary. We carry him with us as a tree does rings. Our growth and his are measured in legends and myths. We see him in the libido forms, and we see him in another way through such bands as the Australoids and various tribes in Africa. What Golding's fiction assumes is that the psychic life of the primitive holds peculiar interest for us, since in it we find an early stage of our own. Golding feels such things in his own bones, rather than in those disinterred. His fiction is intuitive, mythic, and visual.

Through Wellsian fiction the ancient bones come to life. Fossils are evoked to tell their tale. In the process of leading his readers through an imaginative museum of natural history, Wells confesses to finding in the plight of the Neanderthals the "most fascinating of riddles." They followed the unknown Chellean giants but were "perhaps still living in the world when the true men came wandering into Europe." What happened when these early Paleolithic men met later Paleolithic men, our real ancestors? "Almost certainly they met, these grisly men and the true men," Wells writes. "The true men must have come into the habitat of the Neanderthal, and the two must have met and fought." With this as his main assumption, Wells then tries to depict the encounter and its background. The ice was still receding from its last onslaught. The grisly men traveled in small family groups, because there was not enough food during the winter to sustain large tribes. As the thaw came on they left their winter caves and went to the banks of rivers, where flint stones were available.

The true men were more capable of sustaining themselves in larger groups than the Mousterians, because they had better weapons, utensils, and social arrangements. Although they were still savages "prone to violence and convulsive . . . lust," they had laws or at least taboos, and their "moral struggles were ours—in cruder form." They were our kind and understandable as such, Wells declares: "But the grisly folk we cannot begin to understand. We cannot conceive in our different minds the strange ideas that chased one another through those queerly-shaped brains. As well might we try to dream and feel as a gorilla dreams and feels." (If Golding read this piece in Wells's *Short Stories*—and chances are good he did—this opinion about the inscrutability of the sub-sapiens must have been a challenge he could not ignore. Much of the fine artistic achievement of *The Inheritors* is precisely the imaginative way in which he conceives of the "strange ideas that chased one another through those queerly shaped brains."

A hunchbacked, grey, hairy, wolflike monster, with its long arms dangling close to the ground, the grisly man runs in jolting leaps. One of the sub-sapiens in Wells's story watches the grisly folk run, and then imitates them comically, acting the clown. His tribe laughs until tears course down their faces. But subsequent encounters prove less hilarious. Soon after, the tribe of Waugh and Click—the main characters in the Wells narrative—loses a child. A little girl, out picking thistles, has been snatched away—"There was a squeal and a scuffle and a thud, and something grey and hairy made off through the thickets carrying its victim, with Waugh and three of the younger men in hot pursuit." The child is killed; and even though Waugh succeeds in wounding one of the grey monsters with his spear, this first encounter goes heavily against our forebears. Wells imagines that Waugh is in all probability killed, and Click takes over as The Old Man of the tribe. That night Click broods in anger by the fire, haunted by cries of the stolen girl-child. Wells sees all this as "the beginning of a nightmare age for little children of the human tribe."

In turn, however, the grisly folk are doomed. They could not live on very long in "that chill world of pines and silver birch between the steppes and the glaciers after the true men folk came." They are sought out by ones and twos and are killed—"until there were no more of them left in the world." Thus the men folk—with their tools and arts and taboos— become the inheritors. The grisly folk live on only in our archetypal dreams of ogres, accounting for "remote strange experiences in . . . dreams and odd kinks in modern minds."

"A Story of the Stone Age" also appears in Wells's *Short Stories*. It depicts man's continued growth—in killing lions and bear, in taming horses, and in passing on the rule of the tribe through feats of daring and strength. If Golding read it, he could not have found much for his own purposes—at best the feeling of the loneliness experienced by a male and female separated from their tribe, living by their wits, lovingly loyal to each other through all experiences.

But even discounting "A Story of the Stone Age," which is a minor consideration, and thinking only of the *Outline* and "The Grisly Folk," we can readily discern the basic plan for Golding's novel. Wells provided Golding with a scenario in search of character reversal: the good guys and the bad guys are switched around. In *The Inheritors*, the true men folk are shown to be the child-snatchers with cannibalistic tendencies; the Neanderthals are reduced in physical size and represented as hearth-loving people who mourn the loss of their children. How Golding effects the switch—in fact, a *double switch* that no one has as yet noted in print—will constitute much of the analysis to follow; but part of the reversal remains to be discussed under the general heading of influence, this time with respect to the collaborative effort of Joseph Conrad and Ford Madox Hueffer in their own extraordinary version of *The Inheritors*.

The subtitle of the Conrad-Hueffer novel is *An Extravagant Story*, and the book is just that. It concerns a writer of pleasant English countryside novels who has fallen in love with a very strange girl who turns out to be a "Dimensionist," or, to be exact, a "Fourth-Dimensionist." The narrator-protagonist, one Etchingham Granger, at first takes the girl to be a frightfully beautiful and intelligent fraud. She insists on calling herself Miss Granger, and patiently explains their relationship: ". . . your ancestors were mine, but long ago you were crowded out of the Dimension as we are to-day, you overran the earth as we shall do to-morrow." Eventually, humoring her as he says it, Granger begins to get the idea: "I understand," he says, "that you wish me to consider myself as relatively a Choctaw."

High financial shenanigans enter as the book freely mixes science fiction with *roman à clef* elements of international political corruption. Granger's passion for the girl increases until he becomes a willing dupe. A subplot involving the development of Greenland underlines the essential difference between Granger and Miss Granger: the English gentleman stands in relation to the "Esquimaux" as the Dimensionist stands in relation to the English gentleman. Ironically, each despairs over "the high cost of humanizing a lower race." One of the three Dimensionists who appear in the book, a man named

Fox, defects. But Miss Granger holds firm to her purpose to corrupt and break as many mere mortals as she can. Her nascent love for Etchingham Granger she sloughs off as a momentary weakness. She explains her position as opposed to Fox's: "He liked you. . . . So he went under. He grew blind down here. I have not grown blind. I see as I saw. I move as I did in a world of . . . the pictures of men. They despair. I hear groans . . . well, they are the groans of the dead to me." She also announces the reward for her strength and intelligence; quite simply she declares, "I have inherited the earth." The miserable Granger speaks his own epitaph, as it were, when he declares weakly in return: "And I . . . I only loved you."

Thus the novel ends with the beatitudes relegated to the ash heap. Who shall inherit the earth? A new breed according to Conrad and Hueffer—but most certainly not the meek or those who simply love. The inheritance will go to the strong, the intelligent, and the emotionally cold. But—we can hear the combined Conrad-Hueffer voice warning—that does not mean the earth will be a better place for all this "progress." And of course that is the vital point of both novels called *The Inheritors*.

To appreciate *The Inheritors* fully it is necessary to know something about its sources, to see how these sources have been assimilated, and to understand the process by which they have been so transcended as to produce a literary work of considerable power and originality. Although the casual reader can enjoy a Golding novel without bothering about background materials, Golding himself, without being heavily allusive, encourages the critical reader to understand his borrowing tendencies and his reactive attitude. Most remarkable is Golding's ability to assimilate completely the materials he gets from others. No heavy sign of influence remains, no knot of allusion, to clog his own narrative flow or order. He is as smooth as a Shakespeare absorbing Plutarch, and perhaps smoother. Certainly he places less burden on the reader than does a Joyce, an Eliot, or even a Eudora Welty, whose mythic overlays and allusive mosaics demand previous knowledge of sources in order to gain anything like a proper reading, or indeed make initial sense of things. The surface ease of reading Golding helps account for his wide popularity, but it also accounts for the frequent misreadings—or at least confused readings—of his novels, and not always at the lay level.

With the exception of *Free Fall*, his novels all seem deceptively simple to read, and yet even critics of some astuteness have trouble with them—partly because of Golding's compressed style and obliquely visual presentations; and partly because the modern critical reader, once put on a symbolic or fabulistic track, refuses to get off until the end of the line, even though the author may have gone off on a transfer. Golding's fictional switches are subtle and fast, and his writing tends to become cryptic when he speeds up the narrative. As an example of what can happen, one commentator finds the protagonist, Lok, in his "death throe" at the conclusion of *The Inheritors*, "howling his grief for the companions he has lost." This is just not true. At the conclusion of Lok's narrative section (the end of Chapter 11), Golding beautifully echoes a carefully prepared earlier scene in which Lok is shown going to sleep, and another in which the old man, Mal, is laid to final rest. "It [Lok] *made no noise*, but seemed to be growing into the earth, drawing the soft flesh of its body into a contact so close that the movements of pulse and breathing were inhibited." Lok lies thus under a ledge, watched by hyenas until morning, when the sun appears and the ice on the mountains begins to shift with the final ominous rumble. He is to be victim of an avalanche, we infer. But certainly he is not "howling" in his "death throe." If we read that as Lok's end, then we fail to notice how the same ice-shift and rumble connect Lok's position with that of "the new one," the kidnapped child, being taken away by Homo sapiens in a canoe; and, more importantly, we fail to notice that Lok is drawing himself quietly back into mother earth, like Mal he is being taken back into "Oa's belly."

Another commentator sees Lok and his people as being those "heavy, hairy, apelike forerunners of man." Actually, Golding reveals Lok as "a strange creature, *smallish*, and bowed." Lok, as an enemy of Tuami's tribe, may look big to them, since there is a tendency to exaggerate the size of the opposition. And to the casual reader it must appear that any Neanderthal mentioned must be apelike and ogre-big (H. G. Wells's view). But Golding wants his creatures reduced in size (primitive man was probably small anyway) in order to enlist reader sympathy for the "little guy." Thus he reveals them toward the end of the novel as being small, red creatures instead of the grey hulking beasts depicted by Wells.

There are other misreadings of this sort in Golding criticism. One such pushes for a rather plausible symbolism concerning fire and water in the novel, but bases its argument on statements like this, which are not exactly accurate: "Refusing to cross the arm of water that separates them from the humans, they can neither attack their island nor be successful in their attempts at rescue." Lok and Fa do not "refuse" to cross the water; they simply cannot cross. Unable to swim, Lok tries every possible means of swinging himself across the intervening stream, nearly drowning himself in the process. And when at last he and Fa succeed in building a log bridge, their opponents do not elude them. Chances for rescuing Liku and "the new one" fail not because of any hesitancy or fear of water, but because Lok does not understand the situation, nor does Fa until too late.

More importantly, several critics and reviewers have read this book in such a way as to downgrade Lok's people, claiming they are no real match for the intelligence of the Homo sapiens, since their language is clumsy and their thought processes incapable of abstraction. But the downfall of Lok's people comes not so much from lack of intelligence as lack of "education"—*and* from a characteristic good-naturedness that leads them straight toward extinction, with the false assurance about themselves and the Homo sapiens invaders that "People understand each other." Lok's folk are capable of establishing a religion, and even making up sophisticated social epigrams to suit it, such as "A man for pictures. A woman for Oa." Lok eventually deduces what has happened to the missing Ha, and discovers the logical and poetic uses of "like," in the sense of analogy and metaphor.[7] And Fa has a quick enough intelligence to grasp intuitively the possibilities of ransom, when she decides that the captured Tanakil, from the opposing tribe, will bring "the new one" back in exchange.

Taken separately, misreadings of the kind noted here might

[7] Lok, with a burst of insight, discovers that he had been using "likeness" all his life, like one of Molière's characters who is surprised to find that he has been speaking "prose" all his life. But now likeness is something he can really grasp, like a "tool." He so appreciates the beauty of this new tool that he tries it out in order to understand the others, whom he now recognizes as being people also: "The people are like a famished wolf in the hollow of a tree." "The people are like honey trickling from a crevice in the rock." "They are like the river and the fall, they are a people of the fall; nothing stands against them." "They are like Oa."

not seem serious; but they mount up enough to throw considerable darkness over the novel itself. So perhaps it is necessary to outline certain areas of the book—its plot, the nature of the opposing peoples, the intricately worked-out setting—before discussing its technique and theme.

In plot the novel follows the *Outline* and "Grisly Folk" story. Lok's tribe of Neanderthals, referred to simply as "the people," leave their winter cavern by the sea and head toward their summer place in the coastal mountains at the edge of a river overlooking a mighty fall. On their way they must cross a marshy stretch of water, and coming to a place where they have crossed since time out of mind over a certain log, they find the log missing (a log which, the reader subsequently discovers, has been moved by the invading Homo sapiens, later referred to as "the others").[8] Their inland journey provides an important mishap when "the old man" (Wells's designation also) falls into the marsh water and aggravates his already apparent pulmonary disorder, so that he dies within twenty-four hours of reaching their new home site, which they reach only after a torturous climb up the cliff alongside the fall. Hungry and miserable, the people settle down for their first night under their ledge by the river. There are only about six days covered in the book, and this marks the end of the first—with a smell of danger in the air, something which

---

[8] This situation provides an example of how Golding manipulates his materials. The reader understands about the logs only if he pieces together widely separated bits of information—the one coming much later in the novel (p. 171), where Lok, watching the new men build a gigantic fire, offhandedly acknowledges that he "could see part of the log that had killed Mal leaning against the pile"; and the other coming early in the book (p. 13), where Ha examines traces of the old log used by the people; and only then does it become apparent with hindsight that it, too, must have been taken away by the new men.

Lok, as he hunches down into a crouched sleep, cannot place: "He squatted, puzzled and quivering. He cupped his hands over his nostrils and examined the trapped air. Eyes shut, straining attention, he concentrated on the touch of the warming air, seemed for a moment on the very brink of revelation; then the scent dried away. . . ." There is also a sound of danger—"from the foot of the fall, a noise that the thunder robbed of echo and resonance"—but Lok sleeps balanced on his hams: "Frost twinkled on him like the twinkling ice of the mountain."

The smell, noise, and ice mark the ensuing dangers. On the next day, as the people look for food and firewood, one of their members, the thoughtful Ha, falls victim to the invaders whose presence is only now sensed. Then in swift succession Mal dies and is buried; Nil and "the old woman" (she has no other designation) are killed; and the two children, Liku and "the new one" (a babe in arms) are kidnapped. Lok and his mate, Fa, who is a near-victim but escapes, are reunited. They spend the remainder of their efforts in the novel trying to rescue the children, who have been spirited to an island in the river, an island that exists on two levels, above and below the fall, with a land precipice connecting.

Partly by insight and partly by accident, Lok and Fa manage to make a bridge with one log that piles others up in a widening path across the river branch to the upper part of the island and then climb down to the lower level by grasping "roots and the ivy." Here they get only a vague impression of the invading newcomers, because Lok cannot contain himself at the sight of the captured Liku, and his impulsive call to her brings fearful and combative action from "the others." Lok and Fa narrowly escape by fleeing back up the precipice, at whose brink they lie gasping, then across their makeshift bridge to their safe home-place, where momentary relief is tempered by concern over Liku and the new one. They seek solace in themselves: "The two pressed themselves against each other, they clung, searching for a centre, they fell, still clinging face to face. The fire of their bodies lit, and they strained towards it." These events mark the end of the third day.

On the morrow, Lok overrides Fa's plan to leave the children and start their tribe anew (she understands better than he the odds against them). They travel down the edge of the fall to level ground on the river's lower shore, and there, finding a convenient dead tree with a gigantic hollow top, they clamber out of the way of the others, who are leaving the island to set up a new camp. From their observation post, Lok and Fa watch the newcomers and provide the reader with a limited view of "the others" (and of us as humankind) that is rich with irony and fresh with primitive insights. They watch people whom they dub "Pine-tree," "Bush," and "Chestnut-head." They recognize "the old man" of the opposing tribe, and they hold on to the name of one of the others when they hear it uttered as "Tuami." The new people have a peculiar scent, "a sea-smell, meat-smell, fearsome and exciting"; they have black hair which does not cover their bodies completely; they have "a piece of white bone" placed under their eyes (actually the nose); and they have over their eyes a bone that bulges "up and [is] swept back to be hidden under the hair" (the forehead). Here Golding seems somehow to be using the God-given gift to see ourselves as others see us.

On the fourth night Liku is cannibalized, unbeknownst to Lok, who is literally kept in the dark by Fa. Her body trembles in horror as she watches the human barbecue begin: "She knelt up again, pulled him towards her and held his head against her breast while her face looked downwards through the leaves and her heart beat urgently against his cheek. He tried to see what it was that made her so afraid but when he struggled she held him close and all he could see was the angle of her jaw and her eyes, open, open for ever, watching." After the worst is over Lok joins her in watching, their eyes treated to a tremendous orgy of drinking and seduction (of the buxom Vivani by Tuami), their noses assailed by the potent sweetness of the mead-like drink of the new people. When the others are all asleep, Lok and Fa try to retrieve "the new one," but Lok insists on searching for Liku, whose smell ironically permeates the atmosphere (she is on everyone's lips, as it were, as well as on a multitude of camp objects). He disturbs the camp, and the fourth night ends in a shambles.

The new people, apparently terrorized, begin to clear out with the first light of the next day. After portage of their canoes and possessions, they scramble up the mountainside. Fa and Lok watch all this frenzied activity, as Marlan, the chief, whips his people into further exertions; and when the others are far enough away, Lok and Fa fall heir to their leftovers. They drink the remaining alcoholic beverage and Lok declares: "I am one of the new people." Homo neanderthalensis here enjoys his first drunk and suffers, along with his mate, his first hangover.

The story then comes to a close with a rush, like the speeded-up section of a farcical movie—as Lok and Fa make one more effort to rescue "the new one," Fa acting the decoy as Lok makes his way into the midst of the new people. But this fails too: Fa is wounded, the ice begins to move on the mountainside, huge trees come floating down the river, and one sweeps the wounded Fa over the fall. The new people have not fared well either: several of them are swept to their deaths in the stream; they lose one of their canoes when Lok runs through the thong holding it to the mountainside, sending it and other materiel plunging to the bottom land. But Lok is the last of the people, almost, as it were, the Last of the Mohicans, a vanishing people. He searches everywhere for Fa, then for anything companionable, but finds only traces of Liku and the burned remnants of her Oa doll. His howl then seems to announce recognition of what has happened to Liku. He returns to their home cave at the top of the fall, and there curls himself into a furry ball of resignation, right above the spot where Mal is buried, and never even startles at the thunder of the ice-slides on that last morning.

There is an epilogue which concludes the novel and deserves more attention than might be allowed for by the tendency of readers who have been overly moved by Lok's plight to skip it. It is in this chapter (12) and the one preceding it that the greatest chances of misreading occur. Not that there is any "gimmick" to this ending. The first ten chapters in the novel present everything from the viewpoint of the people, that is, Lok's tribe. Lok, Fa, and their relatives are constantly presented in the third person singular. Chapter 11 modulates the narrative point of view. About two-thirds through the chapter the point of view shifts, as Fa goes shooting over the waterfall (*the* fall is represented in physical as well as psychical form) to her death, and it is her death that reduces her mate to the level of an *it*. With her death he is dehumanized. "The red creature," Golding writes for the first time, "stood on the edge of the terrace and did nothing." Then Golding deliberately brings his point home with the insistence of the neuter pronoun *it*, which begins appropriately with Lok contemplating another it, a taboo figure of himself hastily sculpted by Tuami: "It looked at the other figure, dark now, that grinned down. . . . Then it turned away and ran through the little passage that joined the terrace to the slope. It halted.

. . . It turned again. . . . It began to sidle along the path.
. . . It was peering down into the thunderous waters. . . ."
Then the shift in view is completed: Lok is reduced in size
as are the children suddenly at the end of *Lord of the Flies*.
We now see him as the others, the Homo sapiens, have seen
him, as an animal described in words that sound as if H. G.
Wells were writing the passage: "It moved faster, broke into
a queer loping run that made the head bob up and down and
the forearms alternate like the legs of a horse. It stopped. . . .
It put up a hand and scratched under its chinless mouth."

This chapter of transition in which Lok, lover and father,
and family comic, is reduced to an *it* is one of the best things
Golding has written. It has as much power and emotion
(skirting the edges of sentimentality) as that in which Simon
is washed away by the sea in *Lord of the Flies*. When "the
creature" begins to dig around in the fire bed of the true men,
with its weight "on its knuckles" and "its nose lowered almost
to the ground," no true man reading the passage can afford
less than a shudder. "Out of the churned-up earth the right
forepaw picked a small, white bone"—the last remnant of the
much-loved Liku. At exactly this point, where Lok's humanity is our humanity, Golding plunges him ironically into his
most bestial stance: "It was a strange creature, smallish, and
bowed. The legs and thighs were bent and there was a whole
thatch of curls on the outside of the legs and the arms. . . . Its
feet and hands were broad, and flat, the great toe projecting
inwards to grip. . . . There was no bridge to the nose. . . .
Above this again, the brow was a straight line fledged with
hair; and above that there was nothing."

In terms of physical description, of course, we seem to be
reading almost straight Wells—but it is Wells with a ven-
geance and with our sympathies turned topsy-turvy, seeing

the Neanderthal as something more human than man. If it were not for Golding's dispassionate rendering of these scenes, they would become maudlin. He maintains his tone and distance, however, and at the right moment turns to a new and well-prepared-for viewpoint. It has been foreshadowed in this remarkable penultimate chapter, which, although it covers only about an hour's time of action, allows for all hell to break loose, as though someone had given orders to a writer to work as swiftly and economically as a movie camera: arrows, spears, flood, ice tremors, Fa over the fall, canoes wrecked, other people swept away. All done in full colors of failing day. Then, cut to slow time as darkness falls, and as the Last of the Neanderthals cries, mourns, searches out Liku's remains, and alone finally in the family cavern curls up to sleep and die. The question is, though, how would one get the camera to make the fine shift from *he* (Lok) to *it* (Lok)?

The last chapter is only eleven pages long, yet it accomplishes in respect to the life and problems of Tuami's tribe what the first two hundred-odd pages do for Lok's tribe. Golding's compression here is tremendous; Chapter 12 represents in effect "Book II." In "Book I" emphasis is placed from the first paragraph on Lok, engaged in his method of getting from the winter place to the summer place. We see him running with Liku riding his shoulders, holding on to his "chestnut curls." In the last chapter, we concentrate on Tuami and his problems of getting from the river and falls to the upper reaches of a lake. Only five or six days have elapsed since the beginning of the novel, but ages have passed by with respect to man's problems. Lok's people have given way to Tuami's in the focus of the novel. Darkness, thunder, the tremors of shifting ice have replaced "the drifts of vivid buds," which Lok brushed aside as he ran. Liku has been replaced by Tanakil, who lies in a near-coma, victim of the trauma experienced in having seen her primitive friend cannibalized. Fa is dead and so is Tanakil's father, the man Lok had ironically dubbed "Chestnut-head." The parental love of Twal, for Tanakil, supplants that of Fa and Lok for Liku. The "new one" now rides on Vivani's back, holding on to her hair. And the unsettled pictures in Lok's mind give way to the "swirling sand" in Tuami's tumultuous mind.

The usual interpretation of *The Inheritors* offered in various forms by different commentators runs this way: Lok's primitive people live in peace and happiness until they are physically and morally beset by Tuami's more advanced but corrupt tribe. The fall from primitive, Edenic innocence is accomplished symbolically by the introduction of an alcoholic beverage, which Lok and Fa drink. It is not the apple but applejack, as it were, that accounts for their fall: they come to see as the true men do; they achieve sophistication and perdition in one swift orgy. So modern man, or at least his early representative, is the villain, the devil. He introduces sin and a sense of guilt—as well as art, magic, and the sense of taboo—to the scene. Such "true men" may, like Conrad-Hueffer's "Dimensionists," be the inheritors of the earth, but the point is that they are also the corruptors. What price human progress and civilization?

There are several things wrong with this interpretation. The most apparent is that Tuami and his folk have not introduced taboo and a sense of guilt to formerly guilt-free, pre-lapsarian people. First in taking meat from a dead deer, and second in following Fa into the cavern of the "ice women," Lok shows a considerable understanding of taboo and guilt. Although a cat has killed the deer and sucked its blood so that there is no "blame," Lok feels himself in the presence of forbidden things, "with the rich smell of meat and wickedness." And as he carries the meat toward their cavern he has a "brilliant thought" to complete his own exculpation: "The meat is for Mal." Meat—by Lok's own description—has been an enticement before this. There is clearly a history of reverence for all kinds of life on the part of Lok's people, but not a total innocence of flesh-eating. Unquestionably, Lok's people do not see through sensory impressions unmodified by reason, although their ability to understand what afflicts their senses is still so limited that Lok can watch "water run out" of someone's eyes without being aware of the concept of crying.

There is a sense of innocence in the deity of Lok's people, the earth-mother goddess Oa, who is worshipped not by fleshly sacrifice but as Oa appears in natural forms, a root shaped like a woman (a reversal of the more "modern" mandrake-root concept), female-shaped hillocks and ice formations. The religion of Tuami's people is masculine, and sacrificial, but equally totemic, its sophistication arising from the artificial (and sacrificial) nature of some of the totems—a stag inscribed in the soft earth, a man dressed as a stag, the offering to the stag of an amputated finger from a victim chosen by lot. Here is the most clear-cut division between Lok's folk and the new people, who to him are "like the river and the fall . . . nothing stands against them." They are the people of the Fall in more ways than the geography of their origins, for although both peoples *know* evil, only the new ones go beyond the inhibitions to its practice.

The most important fallacy in the sweeping "innocence-corrupted-by-sophistication" reading—the attempt to see the novel entirely in terms of an allegory of the Fall, with Lok a Neanderthal analogue of Adam—is that it ignores Golding's dramatic change of viewpoint in the last chapter of the novel.

The shift is vital. Everything must now be seen from Tuami's angle of vision. His life has changed; his people can no longer go back to the sea, since they believe the "devils" (Lok's folk) guard the river and mountains leading back to the sea. They are no longer the "bold hunters and magicians" who began this inland trip. Tuami believes contact with the devils has given him back a "changed Tuami." And the chief, Marlan, states their position with respect to the devils: "They keep to the mountains or the darkness under the trees. We will keep to the water and the plains. We shall be safe from the tree-darkness." All Tanakil can do is awaken for a few moments from her coma to mutter "Liku," and groan with pain.

Out of all this fear and confusion, Tuami wonders what further sacrifices will have to be made (they have lost most of their people as well as Tanakil's sanity). What, too, he wonders, will happen when the little red devil brought along for Vivani becomes full grown? The people in the canoe watch the creature scamper around Vivani's lush body, watch him (it?) tug at her breasts; and in spite of themselves experience "a well of feeling opened in love and fear." Tuami, who has been thinking of killing Marlan, relents; he stops sharpening the blade of his new knife (see Wells's *Outline* concerning this and other artifacts), and he asks himself: "What was the use of sharpening it against a man? Who would sharpen a point against the darkness of the world?"

These may be the most important words in the entire novel—and the best key to its meaning. They express the lament of the artist. Tuami is the precursor of Sammy Mountjoy and Dean Jocelin, who, like Golding himself, try to fashion an artistic password out of the world's dilemma. That word comes to Tuami when the frightened red devil crawls up behind Vivani as the ice tremors rumble—"Then the devil appeared, arse-upward, his little rump pushing against the nape of her neck." Somehow humor and love are inherent in this, ass-backward as they may be. And perhaps this is the point—the one to be sharpened against the blackness and trembling of the earth. But only perhaps. For as Tuami looks out, at the conclusion of the novel, trying to see ahead, up the lake, he is not able to "see if the line of darkness" has "an ending."

Even if this dualistically sympathetic reading of the novel cannot be pushed far—and Golding skillfully avoids being explicit about this point—the book is much too complicated and subtle to lead us in the ways of the usually offered thesis. Golding's answer to man's position in the universe certainly cannot be so simple as that arising from the idea that primitivistic good is laid low by sophisticated evil. He is certainly not saying with this novel that man should return to the primitivistic Eden, not even were that possible. Nor is he offering Rousseau's noble savage as saint or savior.

On the other hand, Golding does not believe (as Wells seemed to in his early days) that things keep getting better and better. Instead, Golding asks that we look for a point to sharpen against the darkness of the world. That point is not simple faith in evolution, because evolution does not guarantee civilized acts (enter Ballantyne). This is likewise the message of Conrad and Hueffer's *Inheritors*. The heart of darkness can show up in the most advanced as well as the most retarded. Golding wants to focus on the point needed to fend off the darkness. That is the true focus of *The Inheritors*—not simple remorse for the way things once were, or even simple reversal of the Wellsian way.[9]

[9] Golding has provided an interesting link between the generation of his novel and our own, in a review, ostensibly unrelated to Tuami's world. "For the universe has blown wide open," he writes, "[it] is a door from

That Golding has used the artist's way is apparent in his own craftsmanship. He transcends his sources through a style and technique that are both products of his extraordinary power of visualization. He succeeds as a novelist not because he tells a story so well or writes fine dialogue, but because he sees and makes others see. The fact is that he is a sight writer—one who might very well object to, or reverse, Joyce's famous line, in *Finnegans Wake,* written in praise of the oral-aural track: "What can't be coded can be decoded if an ear aye seize what no eye ere grieved for." Golding would have to make it "if an eye ere seize what no ear aye grieved for" to fit his own artistic bent.

More than half the reward of reading any Golding novel comes from donning the necessary glasses and seeing things as the author arranges them in a flow of visual image. But this is especially true of *The Inheritors,* which is a subtle dramatization of the very technique by which the novel is accomplished. Golding here stands as something of an overseer, the reader an inter-seer, Tuami a medial-seer, and Lok, as the father of us all, a base-seer. From the very beginning of the novel Golding gives us pictures as they enter Lok's head; they come as a series of highly colored slides, and are sometimes interchanged and shared among the members of his tribe. The ironic focus in these primitive pictures is such that we understand more of what they mean than do the viewers, especially

which man does not know whether blessing or menace will come. . . . We stand amid the flotsam, the odd shoes and tins, hot-water bottles and skulls of sheep or deer. We know nothing. We look daily at the appalling mystery of plain stuff. We stand where any upright food-gatherer has stood, on the edge of our own unconscious, and hope perhaps, for the terror and excitement of the print of a single foot." Review of *Ring of Bright Water, The Spectator,* September 16, 1960, p. 409.

Lok, who is not the most clear-seeing of his group. But what becomes increasingly ironic is that even we do not comprehend all of what these simple folk see, at least not at the moment of presentation. More pictures are needed, and given, until finally the entire visual apparatus is exchanged for a new one. We go, so to speak, to a new and wider screen, provided through the more sophisticated Tuami; and we learn to focus with hindsight on things seen previously by Lok (who, in turn, has taught us how to look forward toward "the others"), until eventually we get something like the total vision Golding must have intended.

Actually, then, the central fictional problem in *The Inheritors* is visual. Here matters must be shown freshly, somewhat out of ordinary focus, and then revealed in proper narrative perspective. Much the same thing is true in *Lord of the Flies*. If the children of that novel deserve to be considered "men of smaller growth," then the physical adults of *The Inheritors* deserve to be considered children of larger growth; and, in either case, the author must obey the injunction of the Bible and of poetry to be, or see, as little children. It is the problem, say, of William Faulkner telling part of his tale through the eyes and mind of an idiot, in *The Sound and the Fury*. Idiots, children, and Lok's people present much the same problem— how to see things, how much to see, how much to show, and how much comprehension should be allowed at any given point to both the fictional viewer and the reader. In this instance it can be said that Golding does a more realistic job than Faulkner, since Faulkner tries too much to have matters both ways—that is, he seems to narrate from Benjy Compson's viewpoint, but recounts incidents and conversations much beyond the reportorial ken of an idiot. Although Golding avails himself of an overseeing method, seeing things of a background nature which Lok is too preoccupied to notice except in small detail, he sees matters from alongside Lok; and much of the accomplishment of *The Inheritors* lies in the veracity of this maintained view, keyed to the limited possibilities of sub-sapiens vision. Working in this way, looking as far into the blackness of the past as Tuami does into the blackness of the future, Golding accomplishes a great deal. It is enough to make one developmental psychologist graciously and perceptively admit: "Golding beats all the psychologists in his conceptualization and portrayal of a limited mentality combined with an affect life rather fully developed—which is what cultural anthropologists and psychologists would assume about a sub-sapiens level of evolution." [10] Nevertheless, *The Inheritors* must stand as literature, and therefore as art, and as such may answer part of the massive question posed by Joseph Campbell in his *The Masks of God: Primitive Mythology:*

Who will claim to know what sign stimuli smote our releasing mechanisms when our names were not Homo sapiens but Pithecanthropus and Plesianthropus, or perhaps even—millenniums earlier—Dryopithecus? And who that has knowledge of the numerous vestigial structures of our anatomy, surviving from the days when we were beasts (for example, the muscles of the caudal vertebrae that once wagged our tail), would doubt that in the central nervous system comparable vestiges must remain: images sleeping, whose releasers no longer appear in nature—*but might occur in art?* [11]

[10] Professor Dale B. Harris, editor of *The Concept of Development: An Issue in the Study of Human Behavior* (Minneapolis, 1957), in a letter to the authors, December 3, 1963.
[11] (New York, 1959), p. 34. Italics added.

4

SEAMAN PROMETHEUS:

PINCHER MARTIN

The mind is its own place, and in itself
Can make a Heaven of Hell, a Hell of Heaven.
What matter where, if I still be the same,
And what I should be, all but less than he
Whom Thunder hath made greater?

> —*Milton's Satan, in* PARADISE LOST

*N*OT, PERHAPS, since Eliot and his *Waste Land* has a piece of writing resounded with so many significant literary reverberations as Golding's *Pincher Martin* (1956), his third novel. As with *The Waste Land*—to which it may be slightly indebted—its richness of allusion and its echo after echo of our literary and mythic past not only demand repeated readings, but also gain in power from them. Unlike *The Waste Land*, however, which appeals more to literary exegesis than to the mythic memory in man, *Pincher Martin* can be read without a gloss. To the reader with a sense of myth—that of The Fall, or of Job, or Prometheus or Ajax—the tale catches fire. To the reader aware of the literary associations in the background of *Pincher Martin,* the narrative gains in richness and intensity without losing any of its relentless power. In the background of the novel the reader can recognize echoes (deliberately placed there or not) of Bierce and of Hemingway, of Shakespeare's Lear and Milton's Satan, of Eliot and of Conrad—and even of a minor adventure narrative of World War I entitled *Pincher Martin.*

The story seems a simple one. Christopher ("Pincher") Martin, survivor of a torpedoed destroyer, makes desperate efforts to survive, alone, on a barren rock in the North Atlantic. Strong as is his will to live, he cannot survive on will alone. And when we come to the last pages of the tale, we are not sure whether he survived at all, for in the first chapter he seems to have kicked off his sea boots to lighten his weight and stay afloat. Yet on the last page, we discover that his body has been washed ashore with the boots still on.

Paradoxically, Golding's tale is both that of a man's epic struggle for existence and that of a man who is already dead—and who lives only through the last flickering of his will not to be destroyed. Like much of modern writing, it concerns man living at the outermost limit of endurance, on a stage as circumscribed as that of a Beckett or a Pinter, in a situation as circumscribed as Sartre's *No Exit.* Like much of Golding's other writing, it is half allegory, half novel, and has the survival narrative quality and setting somewhat reminiscent of *Lord of the Flies,* even to an epilogue-conclusion in which there is a too-late "rescue" by officers of a nation at war. Again, too, there is a geographical exactitude of description of the tiny island, as with *Lord of the Flies,* although here the details take on a nightmarish clarity and horror, as they do in one of Golding's possible sources—at the least, an analogue—Ambrose Bierce's "An Occurrence at Owl Creek Bridge."

Bierce's tale of the hanging of a Southern officer during the

Civil War opens with the hanging miraculously averted by the snapping of the rope as the victim drops. Or so it seems. Under a hail of bullets Peyton Farquhar swims to safety, and eventually reaches home, where, as he rushes into his wife's embrace, the vision shatters, and the reader understands that his wish-fulfillment episode has existed only in the fraction of a second between the beginning of his not-so-free-fall and the taut rope breaking his neck. Like Golding, too, as Peter Green suggests, "Bierce hints at the illusory nature of Farquhar's experience by heightening his faculties to an extraordinary degree." [1] His physical senses, Bierce writes, "were preternaturally keen and alert. Something in the awful disturbance of his physical system had so exalted and refined them that they made record of things never before perceived. . . . He saw the individual trees, the leaves and the veining of each leaf. . . . He noted the prismatic colours in all the dewdrops upon a million blades of grass. . . ."

Bierce's method has been dubbed, with dubious accuracy, the "post-mortem consciousness." It depends upon a dramatic present, a flash-back, a "post-mortem" period, and a return to the dramatic present, which reveals the protagonist really dead. It is as though the brain, somewhat like hair that seems to grow for a brief period after the body dies, had a life of its own—or something like the chicken's body that cavorts around the barnyard after the head has been chopped off. This kind of ending is as recognizable as the lady-or-the-tiger option. And a quick check of the opening pages of *Pincher Martin* indicates, through a number of strikingly parallel wordings, that Golding may well have looked over the hanging-drowning passage in Bierce's story before he began his

---

[1] "The World of William Golding," *Transactions and Proceedings of the Royal Society of Literature*, 32 (1963), 49.

own. Although memory of the story may have lingered, there is less chance that he returned to Ernest Hemingway's "The Snows of Kilimanjaro," with its dramatic, "post-mortem consciousness" conclusion. In the Hemingway piece a writer, who is much like Hemingway himself, lies dying of gangrene in Africa. He is tended by his "rich-bitch" wife, Helen, with whom he drinks and argues. Through a series of flash-backs he goes over his life and sins, somewhat like Pincher Martin. Finally, as his last night fades into morning, Harry believes that the bush pilot, Compton, has come to take him back to the needed medical attention. He and "Compie" take off for Arusha, Harry's gangrenous leg sticking straight out to one side of the seat in the plane. But instead of Arusha, they head for the fabled top of Kilimanjaro, where everything is "unbelievably white," and Harry believes he is going to the "house of God." Actually, of course, he has never left his deathbed: his stinking leg is hanging off to one side of his cot, the bandages all loose. His wife spots the change with a flashlight and knows where Harry is going, or has gone. He is dead.

Significantly, perhaps, both the Bierce and Hemingway tales are short stories, while *Pincher Martin* is a short novel. Whether the novel's length has flawed its structure has caused some critical controversy. V. S. Pritchett, for example, notwithstanding his earlier praise of the novel, has commented that "*Pincher Martin* is one of the countless instances in modern writing where a novel should have been a short story. . . . Unhappily Golding broke the back of *Pincher Martin* by going into the triviality of the sailor's memories." [2] The chief

---

[2] "God's Folly," a review of *The Spire*, *New Statesman*, April 10, 1964, pp. 562–63. Kenneth Rexroth (*The Atlantic*, *op. cit.*) has a similar complaint: "I object to having to read 185 pages of a worn-out gimmick." Rexroth further sees the reactive nature of *Pincher Martin* with the same

problem about such judgments is that they ignore the fact that excision of the memories, however else it might affect the work, would not reduce it to short-story size. The memories, of course, are a part of the genre of fiction to which Golding's novel is partly indebted.

Golding seems to have left in doubt the conclusion as to whether Martin is experiencing hell or a hellish purgatorial preliminary. The author's own statements on the subject use, often interchangeably, the terms *purgatory* and *hell*, reflecting, perhaps, not authorial inconsistency or irresolution, but a sense of the overlapping of these concepts, for, Golding has said, "Just to be Pincher is purgatory; to be Pincher for eternity is hell." In one of his discussions of the ending of the novel—perhaps, more explicitly, the novel's frame rather than its ending—Golding writes that Martin "is simply in hell. The whole of *Pincher Martin* is Pincher's post mortem experience of himself ('Nothing burns in hell but the self')." Peter Green, quoting these lines of Golding, comments, "From Marlowe to Blake, from Milton to Sartre, echoes of Pincher's self-inflicted purgatory come crowding to the mind." [3] The "Myself am Hell" insight, as Pincher confronts himself—in the seconds he greedily seizes from death—with the facts of his selfish life, seems the only purgatory left to men unwilling to accept classic Christian theology's map of the universe. It is also the only hell. It is significant, then, that the past Martin must review—like a patchily spliced film run too fast, and often too loud—includes events replete with religious suggestion. Even Pincher's expletives continue this train of thought. His friend

---

imprecision of his approach to Golding's first novel: "If *Lord of the Flies* is an unsuccessful attempt to deny *The Swiss Family Robinson, Pincher Martin* is an even less successful denial of *Robinson Crusoe*."
[3] "The World of William Golding," p. 49.

and rival, the saintly Nathaniel, appears in flash-back, and Pincher thinks, "Christ, how I hate you. I could eat you." The eating of Christ (the Eucharist) is clearly a theological heightening of Martin's basic antipathy toward Nathaniel.[4]

The theological clues continue through the novel. Unsubtly on Golding's part, the virginal female whom Martin lusts after is named Mary. Also, in a flash-back about an acting role, Martin recalls doubling as "a shepherd and one of the seven deadly sins." Almost any one of the seven sins could be played by Martin, a friend tells him, "without a mask and just stylized make-up," and he does act out in life that sin always identified with him in the novel, Greed. Greed, writes W. Burnet Easton, Jr., in *Basic Christian Beliefs*,[5] is not so much a sin itself as the external expression of a deeper sin, pride: "The fundamental sin according to the Bible is pride, egocentricity, self-deification, and the insistence that each of us is the final arbiter of what is good for him. . . . It is evidenced in the fact that . . . we seek the good in terms which we, in the privacy of our own selfish judgment, have decided to be good." To make such a judgment, according to this view, is to deny God, and sin becomes "a form of self-deification." It is a final irony for Christopher Martin—one he never fully senses—that although he cannot accept, particularly for himself, either the existence of God or the idea of a heaven, as the novel screams to a close he has a climactic hallucination of the God he has rejected,

---

[4] According to Samuel Hynes, in his pamphlet *William Golding*, "Nathaniel is a religious man and something of a mystic; he lectures on 'the technique of dying into heaven,' and he warns Pincher to prepare for death. Like his Biblical namesake he is a man 'in whom there is no guile'; no doubt we are also meant to recall Christ's words to Nathaniel: 'Hereafter ye shall see heaven open, and the angels of God ascending and descending upon the Son of man." (p. 30)

[5] (Philadelphia, 1957), p. 88.

during which he is obsessed with the concept of heaven: "He knew this before he saw it because there was an awe in the trench, framed by the silent spray that flew over." Although he insists to himself that it is a projection of his own mind, he is compelled to discourse with it, a modern Job with his God. "I have created you and I can create my own heaven," he rages at it. "I shit on your heaven!" It is the final excremental metaphor in a work filled with fecal imagery, and Martin's last words.

The beginning of the novel, like its conclusion, can be better understood from a scrutiny of its possible sources, some buried deep in myth and others more recent in origin. The most recent and personal is undoubtedly Golding's own Royal Navy experience of having been adrift, in wartime, for three days in the English Channel. But there is also H. P. Dorling's novel *Pincher Martin, O.D.* to consider. Dorling, who wrote under the name "Taffrail," published his novel in 1916, and used the naval nickname given to all Englishmen named Martin. Although Golding thought he got nothing from the novel "but the name," a paragraph in Taffrail's novel has a familiar ring. The battleship on which Martin is serving, like the destroyer of Golding's hero, is torpedoed, and the seaman has no choice but the sea:

Life was infallible at that moment and it seemed sheer madness to throw oneself into that seething maelstrom at one's own free-will. Then it was he remembered his heavy sea-boots. Fool, they would infallibly drag him down if he had to swim for it and bending down he kicked his right foot free. He was repeating the process when the end came. . . . He went down and down until his lungs seemed on the point of bursting . . . he was no coward but it was a case of every man for himself and the desire to live was overwhelming. . . . He emitted no sound but a feeble croak, then it was Pincher Martin committed his soul to his maker. He could do no more. . . . It was almost with a feeling of relief that he gave up the struggle as hopeless . . . during this awful time his senses never left him and he found himself wondering how he would die. . . . The most trivial events and the most important happenings of his short life crowded before him onto his over-wrought brain. . . .[6]

Even to the sea boots, Taffrail's novel appears as a direct influence upon Golding; but it is clear also that Golding has reacted sharply against the manner of the earlier Martin's giving up the ghost.

Golding's wide reading is reflected in many of the conscious and subconscious syntheses that appear in his own writings, transformations which seem to indicate the places where disparate literary as well as subliterary works achieve, by a common symbolism, a voice which becomes Golding's own. One of the most striking examples of this means by which Golding acquires a symbolic "voice" which has the quality of myth may have its origin in the cliché ending (as well as the cliché phrasing) of Taffrail, where, "from the very jaws of death, Pincher Martin stepped ashore." Golding's drowning Pincher Martin, who finds the struggle for salvation within himself, finds also the jaws of death—the vast stage of that battle—within himself, when his consciousness of a decayed tooth (perhaps symbolic of his moral state as well) leads the drowning seaman, in his last delirium, to think that he has been washed onto a rocky refuge—"teeth" in his later references. Erroneously, Martin senses in his last instant that he is condemned "to lie on a row

[6] Ian Blake has pointed this out in *Notes and Queries,* IX (August, 1962), 309-10.

of teeth in the middle of the sea"—in Martin's description a gaping mouth we can visualize as a medieval drama's hell gate, "a double barrier of bone. . . ."

T. S. Eliot's Phlebas the Phoenician also dies by water—in the fourth part of *The Waste Land*—and, like the two Martins, "As he rose and fell/ He passed the stages of his age and youth. . . ." And in the fifth part of *The Waste Land*, "What the Thunder Said," a few lines later, we read about waterless rocks (sustaining Eliot's image of sterility), but rocks which are also "Dead mountain mouth of carious teeth that cannot spit. . . ." The decay in Eliot's poem is on a grand scale—in the poet's note "the present decay of eastern Europe"—but the experience of physical and spiritual anguish is nonetheless one which torments Martin on his barren rock, a rock which is no salvation.

Eliot's vision of sterility and of the search for salvation is characterized by the sufferer's thirst, and Golding, in a letter, writes of Martin's thirst in a rare authorial attempt to explain his own symbolism:

. . . to achieve salvation, individuality—the persona, must be destroyed. But suppose the man is nothing but greed? His original spirit, God-given, the *Scintillans Dei*, is hopelessly obscured by his thirst for separate individual life. What can he do at death but refuse to be destroyed? Inhabit a world he invents from half-remembered scraps of physical life, a rock which is nothing but the memory of an aching tooth-ache? To a man greedy for life, tooth-ache is preferable to extinction, and that is the terrible secret of purgatory, it is all the world that the God-resisting soul cannot give up.[7]

[7] Quoted in Archie Campbell, "William Golding: *Pincher Martin*," in *From the Fifties* (BBC Sound Radio Drama Series), ed. Michael Bakewell and Eric Evans (London, [1961]), p. 34.

"Where the hell am I?" Martin asks as he imagines himself washed up on dry land; and Golding answers for him, "A single point of rock, peak of a mountain range, one tooth set in the ancient jaw of a sunken world. . . ." With the mountain range and the rock, and the lone, pain-racked hero, we have gone from the microcosmic imagery of Martin's anatomy to the cosmic imagery of myth. Christopher Martin is more than an individual sailor, suffering on a specific rock, several critics have observed; he becomes a mythic symbol of human endurance. Golding has made this point clearly in one of the storm scenes, where Martin shouts at the thunder, "Hoé, hoé! Thor's lightning challenges me! Flash after flash, rippling spurts of white fire, bolts flung at Prometheus, blinding white, white, white, searing, the aim of the sky at the man on the rock—" He is also Ajax defying the lightning in another line, but in his conniving selfishness he is the earlier Prometheus, and in his punishment, the Prometheus of a later phase in the myth. Martin's prewar reputation was that of a selfish sensualist who grabbed at the best of everything, not worrying about whom he might injure to satisfy his greed. Prometheus, both wise and good (unlike Martin), takes advantage of a dispute he is to judge to indulge himself for the sake of mankind. He is selfish only in mankind's interest, deceiving Zeus into accepting as the divine portion of animal sacrifice the bones and fat, and concealing the flesh for man. For this, and other disloyal behavior, Zeus has Prometheus, in the familiar Aeschylean version of the myth, chained naked to a rock in the mountains of the Caucasus, exposed to the heat of the day and the frost and cold of the night, while—each day—a greedy vulture tears away at his liver. In his stubborn, unyielding defiance while isolated on his rock, Martin is a seaman Prometheus; in character he is an ironic opposite, having lived a life of mean greed, as opposed to the mythic hero's grand-scaled altruism. "I am Atlas. I am Prometheus," Martin cries to the storm, yet all his epic struggle demonstrates to him is his smallness, his insignificance in a brutal, indifferent world. As E. M. Forster has pointed out, there is no Redeemer in Golding's theology. The modern Prometheus must continue to suffer on his rock.

Late in the novel, in Martin's final madness, there are weak echoes of *King Lear*, deliberately weak to convey the dissolution of Martin's will to survive. He rages "weakly" against the storm, considers himself a "Poor mad sailor on a rock," and misquotes Shakespeare to the lightning, wind and rain:

> *Rage, roar, spout!*
> *Let us have wind, rain, hail, gouts of blood,*
> *Storms and tornadoes. . . .*
> *. . . hurricanes and typhoons. . . .*

Martin describes himself self-pityingly in language which might easily characterize the aged, mad Lear on the storm-swept heath: "Now I am thin and weak. . . . My eyes are dull stones—" Lear, in his rage against the storm, does not tax the elements "with unkindness," but cries: ". . . here I stand, your slave,/ A poor, infirm, weak and despis'd old man," with "a head/ So old and white as this."

Lear worries that he is "not in his perfect mind," and like him Martin tries to cope with the realization that he has crossed the boundary into madness. A twentieth-century man, Martin analyzes himself in psychological jargon, with its reassurance that "The whole problem of insanity is so complex that a satisfactory definition, a norm, has never been established." And he babbles on to himself, "Where, for example, shall we draw the line between the man whom we consider to be moody or excitable, and the genuine psychopathic manic-depressive?" Martin's response (Lear is beyond self-help) is to "protect normality" through the forced adherence to a routine of behavior. Eventually he welcomes the consolation of insanity, and like Lear flings himself eagerly into the madman's role, for in Martin's babbling desperation "madness would account for everything." But it is Lear who is redeemed in sanity, love, and peace, albeit at a heavy cost; while Golding eschews the happy ending for a conclusion which, however more controversial, may be truer to nature and human nature.

The geographical exactitude of description by which Golding creates Pincher Martin's rock provides us with details almost sufficient for an end-paper map; yet the topography is only revealed—dramatically—by the ever-enlarging radius of Martin's imagined experience, extended from the trench in which he first "finds" himself trapped. The place names Martin gives to areas of his "rock"—to provide them with a reality—are more sophisticated than those coined by the boys on the island of *Lord of the Flies*, but nevertheless also out of his childhood past. In the case of Martin's rock, however, it is more than the names which are invented—it is the rock's topography, its animal life—and the fact of the rock itself. Peter Green suggests that the setting and theme of *Pincher Martin* may derive from a poem, "Rockall," by Michael Roberts:

> Comforting is sleep, but comfort fails:
> The waves break on the bare rock; the traveller remembers
> Shipwreck, the struggle with the waters, the wild climb,
> Cries of the wind; and then nothing.
> Rockall, two hundred miles west of Benbecula.
> Bare rock, eighty-three feet wide, seventy feet high.
> First seen by Captain Hall, 1810, reported inaccessible
> The last spur on the Great Atlantic shelf. . . .

How shall the mind think beyond the last abandoned islands?
The gulls cry, as they cry in the isles of despair,
The waves break, as they break on Tiree or Foula;
Man is alone, and death is certain.[8]

The poem may have appeared before 1956 in a place in which Golding might have become aware of it; but its first appearance in book form was not until 1958, two years *after* the publication of Golding's novel. There are some striking parallels, and Martin actually does call his imagined rock "Rockall," but perhaps because it is a real rock near the British Isles and familiar to English schoolboys and seamen alike.

"I am netting down this rock with names and taming it," Martin tells himself. "What is given a name is given a seal, a chain. If this rock tries to adapt me to its ways I will refuse and adapt it to mine. I will impose my routine on it, my geography. I will tie it down with names." Man has always attempted to exorcise his fear of the unknown, or of the unexplainable, with the use of familiar names, thus, for example, the christening of diseases by their symptoms, constellations by their shapes. The process of naming places is Martin's conscious effort to convince himself of his intelligence and his sanity, to prevent—or at least forestall—the depersonalization which fear and solitude make almost inevitable. He begins life on the rock in a seaweed-covered trench, and finds that the rock is a series of such crevices and ledges, alternating with shallower ridges which also trap water. Roughly, the rock follows—although Golding does not say so—the conformations of the human brain, a likely phenomenon if the rock itself is only a desperately imagined, toothache-inspired figment of Martin's brain. The rock is covered with washed-up rubble of

[8] *Collected Poems* (London, [1958]), p. 148.

a kind—a warning to the reader—more likely to be found on rocks closer to shore than Martin's deep-sea rock: bones of fish and birds, empty shells of crabs, the claws of a lobster, small stones and sea vegetation. The actual naming is a reaction which follows his rediscovery of his identity disc, hanging about his neck. With a kind of astonishment, indicating how far depersonalization had already gone, he reads his name, and reacts by determining to "survey the estate."

The major part of the rock is separated from a line of lesser sections (a row of teeth, Martin thinks) by gaps of shallow water. His first labeled prominence on the main rock—the Dwarf—is a pillar of stones he raises in the hope that it will look man-made to anyone who might train binoculars on it from a distant ship or plane. (A Promethean gesture, it recalls the work of that outcast Titan in taking some of the earth around him, and kneading it with water, making man in the image of the gods, and upright in stature, unlike baser animals.) The most prominent ledge, nearby, is the Look-out, and the lower ledge near the waterline, the place where he remembers being washed ashore, is Safety Rock. An even lower level, where mussels and other edibles are washed in is Food Cliff, plastered white with dried and moldering remains. Inward from Food Cliff is a higher area where he eats, The Red Lion; and from there to the Look-out is a slope clambered along sufficiently often to be named the High Street. On the other side is Gull Cliff. The three lesser rocks, the row of teeth "diminishing into a dark sea," are—briefly and optimistically—three stations in a row on a London underground journey (Bakerloo and Picadilly lines): Oxford Circus, Picadilly, and Leicester Square. An attempted rain-water reservoir in a low basin in the stone becomes The Claudian. But however familiar the names become to him, the unreal nature of the rock nags at his consciousness. Significantly, he soon forgets his London tube stations, and refers to them collectively only as "the Teeth." For however real the rock's existence becomes as a result of Martin's desire to believe it to be real, it can be mapped out topographically, Golding explains, not by the "tongues that became vast ocean currents" and curve about the rock, but by the tongue in his mouth which curves about the uneven barrier of his teeth. Martin fears sleep, because it is "where we touch what is better left unexamined." He cannot let down his "conscious guard," he understands, for it would be "a consenting to die, to go into complete unconsciousness, the personality defeated." Still, he has a desperate necessity for concreteness, and, in spite of himself, he keeps returning. He identifies his "isolated and decaying rock" with himself, for it is not the rock which is isolated and decaying, so much as it is Pincher Martin himself. Illness and exposure leave him a mass of disgusting, noisome flesh. He suffers from food poisoning and realizes that hell is within oneself. "I am in servitude," he agonizes, "to a coiled tube the length of a cricket pitch. All the terrors of hell can come down to nothing more than a stoppage. Why drag in good and evil when the serpent lies coiled in my own body?" Prometheus has his entrails gnawed at by a carrion bird, but Martin, the modern, do-it-yourself Prometheus, must work at his own entrails, and, improvising from parts of his life belt, inflicts upon himself a crude enema. The remarkable scene is truly dramatic, with more catharsis than even Aristotle would bargain for; and Martin emerges heroically from his agony. He has come as close as man can ever come to outwitting nature by intelligence. We forget his depraved past as much as Golding will let us, but the metaphors of greed are unceasing, and Martin's final hallucination is depicted without compassion. In the storm his body is struck down, and even the quacking mouth dribbles into silence; but the "centre" of instinct survives until the end, and with it, symbolically, a weakening pair of claws—the "Pincher" of Pincher Martin, who has stolen everything in his life.

The final chapter reads like a Conrad epilogue—specifically, like the epilogue to Conrad's *Victory*—where again a Davidson appears on a lonely island to verify the death of the hero. Beyond the island, Golding writes, in an image which could have come out of early Conrad, "the sun sank like a burning ship, went down, left nothing for a reminder but clouds like smoke." Campbell, the crofter on the little island in the Hebrides, has found the body washed ashore, his life jacket significantly still around him. "They are wicked things, those lifebelts," he says, taking his eyes away from the stretcher. "They give a man hope when there is no longer any call for it. They are cruel. . . ."

As a result he worries how long the dead sailor had suffered, and receives Davidson's consolation: "Then don't worry about him. You saw the body. He didn't even have time to kick off his seaboots."

The shock of discovery, in the epilogue, that Martin has not died on the rock after four days' exposure, but drowned at sea soon after he was plunged into the water, has been denounced as trickery and gimmickry—a cheap *deus ex machina* device (though, considering Martin's end, certainly a late machine, at that). It is only a trick to those who have not read the novel carefully enough to catch Golding's frequent and well-planted clues. Although we know Martin has kicked off his sea boots while struggling in the sea, *we find him facing his sea boots in the last wild scenes on the rock.* On a close reading, the end of the first chapter can be taken as an end to consciousness. And almost from the beginning the suggestion is made that the rock has been conjured out of the memory of a toothache, and the tongue's probing of the recesses of the mouth. It is a suggestion made repeatedly through the novel. The nature of what Martin finds on the rock itself fits the coastal strand of his childhood rather than a rocky ocean promontory, and reveals the starved desperation of his imagination, as he clutches the idea of survival. And if we have not been made suspicious of Martin's imagined safety by these evidences, Golding adds throughout the novel crucial incidents of Martin's own horrified realization that his imagination has made a mistake. He sees seals on the rocks known to him as "the Teeth," and realizing his error, cries, "Oh, my God!" He scales a cliff by using limpets as suckers, sees a *red* lobster swimming, lizards flying, forgets that guano is insoluble in water. Realizing the latter, his mind tries to retreat from the thought, but cannot. "If guano is insoluble, then the water in the upper trench could not be a slimy wetness," he realizes in a flash. And immediately there is a horrified physical response:

His tongue felt along the barrier of his teeth—round to the side where the big ones were and the gap. . . . He stared at the sea and saw nothing. His tongue was remembering. It pried into the gap between the teeth and re-created the old, aching shape. It touched the rough edge of the cliff, traced the slope down, trench after aching trench, down towards the smooth surface where the Red Lion was, just above the gum—understood what was so hauntingly familiar and painful about an isolated and decaying rock in the middle of the sea.

At this point in the novel there can no longer be any question about the condition of Christopher Martin, for his horrified thought only reinforces an earlier conclusion Martin refuses to make, and which Golding then explains. "How the hell is it that this rock is so familiar?" Martin asks himself. "I've never been here before—" But he has, and breaks off the dangerous thought when it begins to rise in his conscious mind. Elsewhere in the novel Golding explains why Martin must suppress the realization that the rock "is so familiar":

Familiar, not as a wartime acquaintance whom one knows so quickly because one is forced to live close to him for interminable stretches of hours but familiar as a relative, seldom seen, but to be reckoned with, year after year, familiar as a childhood friend, a nurse, some acquaintance with a touch of eternity behind him; *familiar now, as the rocks of childhood, examined and reapprized holiday after holiday*,[9] remembered in the darkness of bed, in winter, imagined as a shape one's fingers can feel in the air—

Is Martin dead? Certainly he fears so, and cannot quite shut the idea out. "I must have a beard pretty well," he muses. "Bristles, anyway. Strange that bristles go on growing even when the rest of you is—" The instinct for self-preservation makes it impossible for him to utter the fatal word which logically completes the thought. "Like a dead man!" he exclaims at another point; and of course it is true. Realistic as is the surface texture of the novel, beneath it is an allegory of purgatorial experience. The trickery of delayed shock treatment used by Bierce has no parallel here, where the careful reader is prepared all along the way for an inevitable conclusion. The result is that Golding's novel achieves a depth in relation to Bierce's tale equivalent to their settings: the Atlantic Ocean as compared with Owl Creek.

Although the construction of the allegory is subtle, making the conclusion seem a hammer blow, there is no falsity. John

[9] Italics added.

Bowen explains it perhaps too succinctly: "In the short space of time that it takes him to drown, Pincher Martin fights with God, making the affirmation that man can help himself, that man has the equipment to survive and *be* man, and only when everything has failed does he, as an act of will, make his surrender." [10] Bowen, in a later critique, based upon a statement of Golding's, finds a clue to the allegory in Pincher's being summoned by God (the "awe in the trench") by his real name of Christopher in the closing pages of the book. The implication is that Martin's struggle against God is really an internal struggle *with* God, and that he has earned the right to his Christian name, which means *Christ-bearer*. "What could be clearer," Bowen concludes, "than this story of a man being stripped of all he has stolen before he can bring himself to accept, as an act of will, the call of God, the Father? But it is not simple. . . ." [11]

It certainly is not that simple, or that orthodox, for there is no Job-like reconciliation between Martin and the "awe," nor has Martin surrendered; for as Jocelin in the later *Spire* realizes, God "never asked men to do what was reasonable. . . . But . . . out of some deep place comes the command to do what makes no sense at all. . . ." In answer, Pincher Martin, as his agony comes to a screaming climax, cries, "I spit on your compassion!" And when his physical struggle ceases, and the mouth dribbles into silence, "Still the centre resisted," and raged "in a mode that required no mouth . . . voicelessly, wordlessly." Its last conscious thought, we recall, is the defiant "I shit on your heaven!" It is hardly a willed surrender, but the

---

[10] "One Man's Meat, the Idea of Individual Responsibility," *Times Literary Supplement*, August 7, 1959, pp. xii–xiii.
[11] "Bending Over Backwards," *Times Literary Supplement*, October 23, 1959, p. 608.

"awe"—represented by black lightning at the end, and foreshadowed through the novel—wears away the last vestiges of resistance "in a compassion that was timeless and without mercy." This is truly "what the thunder said."

The passing of Pincher Martin is invested with a grotesquely dramatic grandeur which belies Golding's own eschatological analyses of the novel. For *The Radio Times* Golding wrote:

Christopher Hadly Martin had no belief in anything but the importance of his own life, no God. Because he was created in the image of God he had a freedom of choice which he used to centre the world on himself. He did not believe in purgatory and therefore when he died it was not presented to him in overtly theological terms. The greed for life which was the mainspring of his nature forced him to refuse the selfless act of dying. He continued to exist separately in a world composed of his own murderous nature. His drowned body lies rolling in the Atlantic but the ravenous ego invents a rock for him to endure on. It is the memory of an aching tooth. Ostensibly and rationally he is a survivor from a torpedoed destroyer: but deep down he knows the truth. He is not fighting for bodily survival but for his continuing identity in face of what will smash it and sweep it away— the black lightning, the compassion of God. For Christopher, the Christ-bearer, has become Pincher Martin who is little but greed. Just to be Pincher is purgatory; to be Pincher for eternity is hell.[12]

Golding's intentions for the novel are clear—the dramatization of "a modern ego that has not believed in God or an after-life and still adamantly refuses to believe even after it has been exploded into purgatory and confronted by God." [13] But

[12] Quoted by Frank Kermode in "The Novels of William Golding," *International Library Annual*, III, 22.
[13] R. W. B. Lewis in a review of *The Spire, Book Week*, April 19, 1964, p. 1.

Martin comes off better than merely the personification of sheer negation, because of the Promethean intensity of his struggle and the enormous dramatic power which surges through Golding's narrative. As with Milton's heroically fashioned Satan, Golding's Pincher Martin is given an extra magnitude—perhaps beyond that conceived by the writer—because of the writer's own technical resources. Pincher Martin may have made the wrong moral choices, and may be condemned for ignobility of soul, but his is a soul not easily extinguished. Shrunk at the close to a frenziedly resisting pair of lobster-red claws, Martin retains to the end the last vestiges of his personality. To the end, he repudiates mortality.

Are these reddened hands (vestiges of the red lobster Pincher saw swimming near his rock) made red as lobsters ordinarily are changed in color by being boiled? Earlier, the vision of the erroneously red lobster may have been merely another clue to Pincher's conjuring up his island out of need for it—and a clue to augment our distrust of his survival. Is Golding suggesting Martin's final immersion in the fires of Hell?

Sam Hynes, in an essay, "Novels of a Religious Man," sees in the symbolism of Martin's end not only the attempt of a soul to survive before God, but "the torments of a soul as it is stripped to its essential nature—symbolized for Pincher Martin by the terrible lobster claws. . . . The rock and the lobster claws are Pincher Martin's eternity." [14] The claws recall to us Eliot's Prufrock, who, in his despair, wishes that he were "a pair of ragged claws/ Scuttling across the floors of silent seas." It is Martin's ironic fate to have succeeded. The intricacy and intensity of the symbol of the rock Martin creates go, perhaps,

[14] *The Commonweal*, 71 (March 18, 1960), 674–75.

even farther than that of the lobster claws, for the rock is another kind of eternity as well. It is the Rock of Martin's spurned Christian faith, the Rock of T. S. Eliot's early religious drama, where the poet writes that "good and ill deeds belong to a man alone, when he stands alone on the other side of death. . . ." In a few lines in Eliot's *The Rock*, we have a further suggestion of Golding's concept:

The soul of Man must quicken to creation.
Out of the formless stone, when the artist united himself with stone,
Spring always new forms of life, from the soul of man that is joined to the soul of stone. . . . [IX]

The Scriptural darkness that is over the face of the deep, an image repeated often in Eliot's poem, takes a number of forms in Golding's novel, not all of them susceptible to easy analysis: the black lightning that is "the ultimate truth of things," the destroyer of the "carefully hoarded and enjoyed personality"; the interior of the black lacquer Chinese box, perhaps the most concise merging of the concepts of darkness and greed. One of Martin's victims had described, in telling the parable of the Chinese box, how the Chinese would prepare an exotic dish by burying a tin box containing a fish. As the fish decomposed, it would be devoured by maggots. Then, in the darkness of the box, the maggots would devour one another, until, at the end, "where there was a fish there is now one huge, successful maggot. Rare dish." Pincher remembers, and cries, on his rock, "I'll live if I have to eat everything else on this bloody box!"

The black Chinese box strikes a note of deep horror. Also black, and filled with connotations of terror, is Martin's memory of the cellar in his childhood home, a fearful "well of darkness," which Golding has explicated in a letter to a critic as suggesting "that God is the thing we turn away from into life, and therefore we hate and fear him and make a darkness of him." [15] In the novel itself, Golding continues, the cellar's darkness is—although the child cannot know it—"the thing he turned from when he was created." Such intimations produce darker clouds of glory than those Wordsworth saw.

Perhaps, as here, Golding's technical virtuosity has led him to load his language with more intended significance than it can reasonably bear, but his intention is always to write novelistic prose which has the emotional and intellectual intensity of poetry; and the sharp particulars of his novel are often memorable images:

Hunger contracted under his clothes like a pair of hands.

A thought was forming like a piece of sculpture behind the eyes.

The dark, lavatorial cleft, with its dripping weed, with its sessile, mindless life of shell and jelly was land only twice a day by courtesy of the moon.

The sea no longer played with him. It stayed its wild movement and held him gently . . . like a retriever with a bird.

The magnified sense impressions—reminiscent of the nightmarish Biercean "Owl Creek"—include unforgettable descriptions of what V. S. Pritchett calls "the roaring, sucking, deafening sea." Golding is a modern writer in *Pincher Martin*, Pritchett adds, "in that his eyes are pressed close to the object, so that each thing is enormously magnified. We see how much a man is enclosed by his own eyes. The important quality of all Golding's descriptions is that they are descriptions of move-

[15] Letter to John Peter, quoted in "Postscript (to 'The Fables of William Golding')," *William Golding's 'Lord of the Flies': A Sourcebook*, ed. William Nelson (New York, 1963), p. 34.

ments and continuous change and are marked by brilliant epithets. (One remembers: 'three prudish anemones.')" [16] Golding, it becomes clearer from book to book, is essentially a visual writer, and what he captures in *Pincher Martin*, as earlier in *Lord of the Flies* and in *The Inheritors*, is what he called with reference to another "castaway" book (*The Swiss Family Robinson*), "the brilliantly evoked spirit of place (the crystal cavern, the lobster pools, the grove of trees); the details held up to the eye and exactly observed (the tools and weapons, the plants and rocks, the good, earned meals). . . ." It was exactly what he found wrong—rereading it as an adult—with *Treasure Island*, where he found "the physical patch of land" not wholly in focus. "We get glimpses that are superb," he has noted, "but the island as it stuck out of the sea, the reason for its being there, and the relationship between the parts, escapes me even when I use the overrated chart. An island must be built, and have an organic structure, like a tooth." [17] To sustain his point, Golding seems to return here to his own central geographic metaphor in *Pincher Martin*.

Other than the imagery surrounding the evocative tooth, there are two major types of metaphors in *Pincher Martin*. The first—an extension of Golding's wordplay on Martin's nickname—are the recurrent metaphors of eating, implying every kind of animal greed and acquisitiveness, from the dietary to the sexual. The second are the excremental metaphors so common to Golding's fiction, here an intensifying fecal imagery which reaches a climax in the explosive scene of Martin's makeshift self-enema (a scene Aldous Huxley might have envied), and a conclusion in Martin's unvoiced "I shit

[16] "Secret Parables," *New Statesman*, August 2, 1958, p. 146.
[17] "Islands," a review of new editions of *The Swiss Family Robinson* and *Treasure Island*, *The Spectator*, June 10, 1960, pp. 844-45.

on your heaven!" challenge to the "awe in the trench." Earlier, the limpets, under his knife, bleed "salty, uretic water," and a procession of vividly disgusting urinary and fecal metaphors follows through the novel. They almost certainly represent man's disgusting humanity. "Why drag in good and evil," we recall Martin telling himself in the enema scene, "when the serpent lies coiled in my own body?" We are reminded of another serpent, of the myth of man's Fall (which Golding had written about before, and to which he returns again in his later books), and of the continuing domination of man by the serpent within him, the bestial side of his nature which to Golding has depraved man since he left the dark cellar of his prehistoric past and "the thing he turned from when he was created." What survives us when we return to the darkness, we who, in Yeats's words are "sick with desire/ And fastened to a dying animal/ It knows not what it is . . ."? [18] Are we, in our disgusting depravity, even worth the thought? The sharp focus of Golding's intelligence and the grandeur of his imagery play upon such questions in a novel which paradoxically quickens our admiration for the heroic tenacity of the human spirit.

To critic John Peter, *Pincher Martin* seems, "in all seriousness, as brilliant a conception as any fable in English prose." But he quickly adds that the book transcends "the mode of fable itself," organized as carefully as a poem, its compelling symbols "integrated into a pattern . . . where the meaning is difficult to exhaust." [19] With its final ambiguity of theme as well as form, *Pincher Martin* will always pose a problem for the individual reader: Do we take the author's word and be-

[18] "Sailing to Byzantium."
[19] John Peter, "The Fables of William Golding," *Kenyon Review*, XIX (Autumn, 1957), 589.

lieve this to be a book concerned with man's disgusting nature and his illimitable pride, or do we go beyond his word to the work itself and find there as well, in the central drama of the novel, the heroic struggles of one lone miserable being, trying to establish his own rock of existence?

5

DOUBLE VISION:

FREE FALL and *THE FALL*

"It's too late now. It will always be too late.
Fortunately!"

   —Clamence, in Albert Camus's THE FALL

GOLDING HAS OBSERVED that writers, sometimes without realizing it, succeed in making language rise above its usual capacities and thus communicate moments of true art. Although this "meta-linguistic effect" is most often ascribed to poets, Golding carefully explained—in speaking before a convention of teachers [1]—that he was not talking about effects limited to poetry. (Had he thought in terms of his own work, he might have immodestly pointed out *Pincher Martin* as an example of a novel possibly enriched beyond its original aims by the writer's technical resources.) Speaking of the eloquence

[1] National Council of Teachers of English address.

of the unsaid as much as the said, in both fiction and other literary forms, Golding mentioned the meta-linguistic effect (in translation, at that) of *Huckleberry Finn* on a Russian writer who, although far removed from Twain in space and time, was nevertheless inspired into a career as a novelist by the excitement of Huck's adventures of moral choice on the distant Mississippi.

To further exemplify and give substance to this point, Golding referred to two other writers, one English and the other French—both of whom dealt with similar subjects and characters, seduction and the necessary twosomes—Samuel Richardson and Choderlos de Laclos. Golding showed how the Englishman, a haberdasher who wrote letters for the girls working for him, was, on the printed page, at least, more conversant with the human heart, while Choderlos, a retired militarist, was more conversant with tactics. In the English novel, Lovelace announces his conquering the titular Clarissa in one poignant, epistolary sentence. In the French novel (again an epistolary effort) *Les Liaisons Dangereuses*, the seducer gives every detail of his climactic overcoming of the good lady. Golding saw the force of Richardson's long novel compressed into the single sentence, filled partly with male triumph and partly with remorse. And in the success of this achievement he found the meta-linguistic effect.

Through such discussions, and interviews, as well as prefaces and autobiographical notes, Golding reveals himself as being more sophisticated and eclectic than some of his admirers—who see him as an ex-Navy schoolmaster interested in children's literature—give him credit for being. Thus it should be no surprise that another English novel, his own *Free Fall*, is susceptible to comparative study with another French novel, Albert Camus's *La Chute*, or *The Fall*. There is much more similarity involved than the obvious connection of the titles. It is quite apparent that Golding has, once again, worked in reaction to someone else's fiction, this time to a novel published and translated into English only three years before the publication of his own novel. *The Fall* was published in 1956, and clearly had fresh impact on *Free Fall*, published in 1959.

Both novels are confessions, or *récits*, both told quite naturally in the first person singular (Golding's only work done in this manner), both concerned with very able and egregious protagonists, both full of sensuality and seductivity, both concerned with the question of how grace or freedom of will has been lost, both theological in allusion and implication, but each reaching a quite different answer through different fictional and moral emphases.

Free Fall and *The Fall* might both have been called by the Camus title—might have, but for Golding's scientific background; for Golding's title has both theological and scientific connotations. Not only does Golding's title remind us more clearly than Camus's of the freedom of will involved in Adam's choice (and all men's), but also of the state of free fall in which man in a condition of neutralized gravitational pull in space is beyond the control of his own direction and acceleration—unless he chooses to apply the techniques available to him to regain that control. The scientific reference emphasizes man's freedom of choice, his freedom of will, his responsibility for his acts.

Free Fall and *The Fall* are both better seen for what they are, in terms of their authors' creative techniques and abilities, as well as their intrinsic literary worth, when placed side by side. As Golding says of his character Lok, in *The Inheritors*, we must become familiar with "like." How is *Free Fall* like *The Fall*? And how not?

The narrator and protagonist of *The Fall* is Jean Baptiste Clamence, a former defense lawyer in Paris, who describes himself now, self-exiled in Amsterdam, as Judge Penitent. After offering his services as an intermediary and guide, he begins his confession, or *récit*, to a man whom he has approached in a bar. Throughout the confession he refers to his unnamed auditor, whose questions are sometimes echoed but never directly heard, as *mon cher compatriote*. The confession takes place in several stages—in the bar, near the Zuider Zee, under a doorway in the rain, and finally in Jean Baptiste's room. The implications of the story are almost completely foreshadowed during the first leave-taking, between confessor and auditor:

Till tomorrow, then, *monsieur et cher compatriote*. No, you will easily find your way now: I'll leave you near this bridge. I never cross a bridge at night. It's the result of a vow. Suppose, after all, that someone should jump in the water. One of two things—either you do likewise to fish him out and, in cold weather, you run a great risk! Or you forsake him there and *suppressed dives* sometimes leave one strangely aching.[2]

The narrator is himself strangely aching. His fear of water immediately places his given name of Jean Baptiste in an ironic light—a strange John the Baptist who cannot save with baptismal water, who cannot himself take the plunge. Actually, his fear of water and low places constitutes the central mystery of his character and life.

It was a life of great promise. Jean was born of respectable but humble family, son of a military officer. Nevertheless, at certain times, he felt "like a king's son, or a *burning bush*."

[2] The version referred to throughout this chapter is the Justin O'Brien translation of *The Fall* (New York, 1956).

From these circumstances he rose to become a renowned Parisian defense lawyer. In this role he abominated judges and the law, but threw himself wholeheartedly—or, rather, *not* wholeheartedly, but eloquently and successfully, nonetheless— into good causes, specializing in the cases of needy widows and orphans and particularly those of murderers. He was magnanimous in helping infirm people cross the streets of life. Nothing gave him more pleasure than kissing the hand of some poor woman whose husband he had just saved, cutting short her thankful effusions and breaking away. Such acts, he confesses, marked the "supreme summit where virtue is its own reward." He is a man who loves summits and abominates the lowlands—whether topological, social, or intellectual. He constantly punctuates his narrative flow with asides like "Let's pause on these heights" or "Now you understand what I meant when I spoke of aiming higher" or "Then I grow taller, *très cher*, I grow taller, I breathe freely, I am on a mountain. . . ."

Yet the peculiar and ironic fact is that he has fallen. His confession concerns primarily *la chute*, the fall. And he sees "the necessity for a certain mortification" in exiling himself to the lowlands of Amsterdam—a city of fogs and canals, by a nearly dead Zuider Zee, a flatland of ashes (shades of *The Waste Land*), a flabby sort of Dantesque hell, as he describes it. How has this man who loathes low places come to this place? How has a man absorbed in the "I, I, I" pinnacle of life, a man of fulfillment and success, fallen so low? He confesses—even as he describes his life as lawyer, protector, doer of outwardly good deeds—to taking satisfaction only in alcohol and women: "Despairing of love and of chastity," he chooses debauchery. But this is not what has lowered him. He was in a German prisoner-of-war camp, and, raised to the camp role of "pope," he drinks water that others sacrifice (in one case with a life) for his sake. But this is not what produced his fall. He is an atheist and confesses to not having been able to take life seriously. But, again, this produced no fall. These things are all before and after the fact.

His fall starts with a certain evening. Tantalizingly he makes mention of it, but keeps putting off his auditor and the reader with remarks that constitute something of a refrain: "What? What evening? I'll get to it, be patient with me." And "What? I'm getting to it, never fear." Eventually he discloses how his own fall is directly connected with the physical fall of someone else. Telling of this almost exactly halfway through the *récit* makes all the rest of his confession, his additional sins, his loss of pride in freedom, tumble out heapingly for the seeming benefit of his *cher compatriote*. His real fall occurs one particular November evening as he returns to his home from the house of one of his mistresses:

I was returning . . . by way of the Pont Royal. It was an hour past midnight. . . . On the bridge I passed behind a figure leaning over the railing and seeming to stare at the river. On closer view, I made out a slim young woman dressed in black. The back of her neck, cool and damp between her dark hair and coat collar, stirred me. But I went on. . . . At the end of the bridge I followed the quays. . . . I had already gone some fifty yards when I heard the sound . . . of a body striking the water. I stopped short, but without turning around. Almost at once I heard a cry, repeated several times, which was going downstream. . . . The silence that followed . . . seemed interminable. I wanted to run and yet didn't stir. . . . I told myself that I had to be quick and I felt an irresistible weakness steal over me. I have forgotten what I thought then. "Too late, too far. . . ." or something of the sort. . . . Then, slowly under the rain, I went away. I informed no one.

He is telling someone now, though. And the question is: Why? There are only two basic reasons for confessions: one is to seek forgiveness and the other is to gain vindication. As we soon find out, in his eventual effort to subvert his *cher compatriote*, who turns out to be another lawyer from Paris (although no one has suggested the auditor as a mirror image of Clamence himself, it remains an interesting possibility), Jean Baptiste is not seeking forgiveness. He has made this confession before and through it lured confessions from others. The more he confesses, the more his auditors eventually confess. And thus through them he gains ascendancy, as over and over again he substantiates his thesis of universal guilt. "Then please tell me," he finally invites his fellow lawyer, who has hardly had a chance to get a word in edgewise—"what happened to you one night on the quays of the Seine and how you managed never to risk your life." Tell me, in other words, what is your great sin, for we have all fallen, are all guilty. As for redemption, Jean Baptiste is having none of it. His last name, Clamence, is not far from *clémence*, but with him, as Judge Penitent, there is no forgiveness. "With me," he declares, "there is no giving of absolution or blessing. Everything is simply totted up, and then: 'It comes to so much. You are an evil-doer, a satyr, a congenital liar, a homosexual, an artist, etc.' Just like that. . . . I am for any theory that refuses to grant man innocence and for any practice that treats him as guilty. You see in me, *très cher*, an enlightened advocate of slavery."

Here lies open at last Jean Baptiste's motive for confession—not, certainly, to obtain forgiveness, or even simply to gain vindication, but to enslave and entrap, to gain ascendancy, to reach the heights once more in the only way remaining, by having others accept his theory of universal guilt, to have them confess, to make them his slaves. *The Fall* is not an easy book to interpret, but it hardly seems possible that Camus was advancing Jean Baptiste as a true rebel or existentialist. We see in him a man who has become *engagé* after having seen his true moment, and, in short, having found himself afraid. He could not enter into the life or the lifesaving of others. Now his *engagement* is a perverse farce, a travesty. He has reached the moral position or essence of Satan—or at least Jack the Ripper. And yet—and yet he makes the reader, his *cher compatriote*, examine his own conscience and past to find *la chute*. The book is not without its ambiguity of effect.

The narrator and protagonist of *Free Fall* is Sammy Mountjoy, who describes himself as the owner of many hats or personalities, but particularly as being *the* Samuel Mountjoy, the well-known artist who hangs in the Tate Gallery. He is trying to trace his true self through the form of a free confession, one lying somewhere between the psychoanalyst's couch and the Catholic confessional box. He hardly knows to whom he is confessing. "With whom then?" he asks somewhat bewilderedly. "You?" And who is that? "My darkness reaches out and fumbles at a typewriter with tongs. Your darkness reaches out with your tongs and grasps a hook."

The narrator—in search of his proper hat or personality or self-with-soul—communicates his present state of being in the very first paragraph of the novel. It encapsulates the essence of his story:

I have walked by stalls in the market-place where books, dog-eared and faded from their purple, have burst with a white hosanna. I have seen people crowned with a double crown, holding in either hand the crook and flail, the power and the glory. I have understood how the scar becomes a star, I have felt the flake of fire fall, miraculous and pentecostal. My yesterdays walk with me.

They keep step, they are grey faces that peer over my shoulder. I live on Paradise Hill, ten minutes from the station, thirty seconds from the shops and the local. Yet I am a burning amateur, torn by the irrational and incoherent, violently searching and self-condemned.

The paragraph is lush and stylistically overwrought, but it is meant to be an epigraphic tone poem summarizing the book, indicating its mystic search and its allegorical mode. In this sense, it is more than acceptable, it is useful; and it takes on a glow of power if reread as a conclusion.

Samuel is the chosen but misunderstanding servant of God; Mountjoy is one who would climb to the desired heights of Jean Baptiste Clamence—or who has, like him, often mounted the *Mons Veneris*. Sammy has traveled quite some distance from his beginnings as a bastard born in a place called, with Bunyanesque bluntness, Rotten Row,[3] a place of fogs and bogs in the cloacal sense. Somewhere in his climb to Paradise Hill Sammy has, of his own free choice, fallen. And the question of what makes Sammy fall becomes the central mystery of his story. His confession becomes a search punctuated by the thematic refrain of "When did I lose my freedom?" Like Clamence, he delays his answer. Time after time, as he puts his life together through a series of time-shifts from the narrative present, Sammy tells his auditor, "Not here," until eventually the point of his free fall is reached.

Sammy confesses to never having known a father; but the

---

[3] Rotten Row, now a reference to a road in Hyde Park, London, was a name once applied to various streets in other English towns as well, and is popularly assumed to derive from *route du roi*; if Golding is using it in the sense of a *double-entendre*, it takes on added meaning in respect to Sammy's mother's "throne" in the bog, and in respect to the Kings of Egypt, who dominate Sammy's boyhood imagination.

opportunity is left open for him to feel, as does Clamence on occasion, that he is descended from royalty (he is constantly preoccupied with some picture cards, obtained while he was just a child, depicting the kings of Egypt; somehow these kings have become fixed in his mind as the apotheosis of glory). When he asks his mother who or what his father was, she answers variously, offering him everything from officers in the Royal Air Force to the Prince of Wales himself. Whoever or whatever his father, Sammy has become a "burning amateur" and his mother seems his only source of being. He sees her as a mother-earth figure, as a terminus associated with their "bog," or outdoor toilet, in Rotten Row. There is a hilarious scene in which his mother prevents another woman from using her bog; it is sacrosanct to her. He sees his mother as the cloacal source of himself, as the end of a tunnel, blocking the view back: "She is the end of the tunnel. . . . Ma spreads as I remember her . . . her wide belly expands, she is seated in her certainty and indifference *more firmly than in a throne*. . . .[4] She looms down the passage I have made in time."

Sammy's fall, however, is not related to his being decanted from his mother or his passage through childhood in Rotten Row. Childhood has its own protective innocence. Even watching sexy little Evie urinate standing up, like a boy, able somehow to send her stream higher up the bog wall than any of the competing boys, Sammy enjoys the exemption from guilt of childhood. Even when, somewhat later, on a dare with another boy, he tries to desecrate a church altar by urinating on it, and is able (after carefully draining his bladder before entering the church) only to expectorate rather dryly—even

[4] Italics added.

under these circumstances he is still innocent, guiltless of any sacrilege by virtue of his animalistic state of childhood. In looking back at this childhood self, Sammy asks the question "Here?" and answers with absolution, "Not here." He acquits the boy in the ward. He belongs with Lok in *The Inheritors* before the coming of Homo sapiens.

After his mother dies, Sammy must be adopted by Father Watts-Watt, live next to the church he mildly desecrated, attend school under the benevolent direction of Nick Shales (scientific rationalist) and Miss Rowena Pringle (sanctimonious Christian bitch), and meet Beatrice Ifor—before he is ready to swoop down in free fall from God and Paradise. Sammy in school is attracted to Nick Shales (whose Satanic name belies his personal goodness, but indicates that for Sammy he is nonetheless tempter). Sammy is repelled by the personal evil and animosity of Miss Rowena Pringle, who, although she makes religious stories come alive for him, also makes his personal life a minor hell, partly because she cannot stand his drawings or his intellectual curiosity, but mainly because she had hoped to marry Father Watts-Watt before Sammy's being adopted thwarted her plan. She sadistically takes out her frustrations on the boy. She accuses him of reading smut into the Bible on one occasion. And she rewards his ability to draw by sending him to the headmaster to be punished for a landscape sketch which, when held a certain way, depicts private aspects of the human anatomy. The headmaster is first confused, then angry, then finally amused and impressed by Sammy's artistic endeavors. He grants him immunity, allowing Sammy to follow his natural talent rather freely, except in Miss Pringle's class. Eventually it is the headmaster who, upon Sammy's graduation day, gives him a vital piece of advice. He knows Sammy to be intelligent and talented but also dishonest and selfish. Despairing of outlining any path toward happiness, the Headmaster erects this sign of recognition and warning:

"I'll tell you something which may be of value. I believe it to be true and powerful—therefore dangerous. If you want something enough, you can always get it provided you are willing to make the appropriate sacrifice. Something, anything. But what you get is never quite what you thought; and sooner or later the sacrifice is always regretted."

Narratively, though not chronologically, this advice is delayed; it comes only some twenty pages from the end of the novel. By this time we have already followed Sammy through numerous selfish acts and peccadilloes. We have watched him try on a Communist hat and take on a wife, Taffy. We have watched him unsuccessfully struggle to erect a bridge between Nick's presentation of physical laws, in respect to conservation of energy, and Miss Pringle's presentation of Moses' burning bush and its metaphysical energy. We have seen him brought to the point of almost betraying himself and his comrades as he is tortured in a German prisoner-of-war camp. We have seen him entrap, seduce, desecrate, and destroy a beautiful, if somewhat weak-minded, girl, Beatrice Ifor. In all instances, except the last, Sammy has raised his anguished question of "Here?" and answered "Not here." In respect to Beatrice the question is raised but left unanswered.

Beatrice Ifor is a beautiful young girl in school with Sammy whom he always sees as with a halo around her lovely head. Her name, within the heavenly allegorical strategy of the book, brings Dante's Beatrice to mind, along with the disjunctive elements of choice—*If-or*. As with Clamence, Sammy reaches his downfall through the actual fall of another person, again a girl. Carefully Sammy lays his traps and finally catches his cony. She falls under his wiles, and he debauches her with every feasible manner of sexual debasement, only to break his promise and marry another girl. Actually, Sammy has fallen because of Beatrice, but before the actual seduction, in a watery bower-of-bliss scene which follows right after the headmaster's advice on graduation day. Alone he makes his way from school to the escarpment of the river nearby; it is a day of days: "Even the wood-pigeons co-operated . . . they sang from their green penthouses and all the forest, the bracken, the flies and uncatalogued small moths, the thumping rabbits, the butterflies . . . they murmured sexily for musk was the greatest good of the greatest number." In the woods he is touched by fronds and feels "a powder spilled out of all living things." He feels hot and sticky, and the water seems to wait for him below. So he strips and plunges in, experiencing his skin, his shape as a man, knowing how "to sow my seed from the base of the strong spine." Out of the water, he once more asks himself what is worth sacrificing for, and the answer comes out "Beatrice Ifor." What will he sacrifice for her white, unseen body? The next-to-last word in this section of the book gives answer: "Everything." The last word is "Here?" And there is no answer, except what the auditor of this confession cares to supply. Sammy's free fall is managed out of free will and occurs here within the budding grove. The sullying of Beatrice is after-climax.

The tortuous scenes of Sammy in a prisoner-of-war camp are anticlimactic, too, although the reader has no way of sensing this. Even if he did he would eventually see that they are necessary. At the very end of Camus's *The Fall*, Jean Baptiste offers himself and his auditor a second chance: "You yourself," he declares, "utter the words that for years have never ceased echoing through my nights. . . . 'O young woman, throw yourself into the water again so that I may a second time have the chance of saving both of us!' " But he sees this as a bitter satire on the nature of things, and concludes: "A second time, eh, what a risky suggestion! Just suppose, *cher maître*, that we should be taken literally? We'd have to go through with it. Brr . . . ! The water's so cold! But let's not worry! It's too late now. It will always be too late. Fortunately!" Sammy's experience in prison and his attempt to help Beatrice, who has been committed to a mental institution, are connected parts of his second chance.

Dr. Halde (whose name means slope in German, and thus the way down, or up) is the psychoanalytical expert in mental torture and extraction of information who supervises the interrogation of Sammy about an attempted escape by his comrades. Halde is somewhat like Jean Baptiste Clamence, witty, intelligent, intellectual. He confesses that he himself has erred several times in his life, even been part of the Communist party. He seeks to establish a human camaraderie between himself and his prisoner, hoping to get him to confess also, since there is nothing (he assures Sammy) that is worth suffering for. When Sammy fails to comply, mainly because he knows nothing of the plot to escape, Dr. Halde, who has studied him carefully and understands his peculiar weaknesses and phobias, has him put in a special cell.

Sammy's cell contains literary echoes not only of Poe's "The Pit and the Pendulum," Orwell's *1984*, Golding's own *Pincher Martin*, but particularly of Camus's *The Fall*, in which descriptions of two very special cells of torture are detailed. The first of these Clamence calls the cell of "little-ease." Probably an actual medieval invention, he considers it a work of genius, because its torture is exquisite and its method quite simple:

"That cell was distinguished from others by ingenious dimensions. It was not high enough to stand up in nor yet wide enough to lie down in. One had to take on an awkward manner and live on the diagonal; sleep was a collapse, and waking a squatting." In such a cell Jean Baptiste believes all men and innocence must collapse: "What? One could live in those cells and still be innocent? Improbable! . . . That innocence should be reduced to living hunchbacked—I refuse to entertain for a second such a hypothesis." The second cell is the "spitting-cell," so arranged that the inmate must stand up facing the door, which reaches up to his chin. Only his face is visible from outside, and every time a jailer passes he spits copiously into the face. "The prisoner," as Clamence adds, "wedged into his cell, cannot wipe his face, though he is allowed, it is true, to close his eyes." [5]

Sammy's humiliation and terror are also matters of dimension and wetness. He crawls around his tiny cell trying to discover just how large it is and what terrors it contains. Certain passages in his thought process give evidence of how fresh in mind Camus must have been as Golding wrote his novel. For example: "Who could have told me . . . that the darkness before my blindfolded eyes would take on the likeness of a wall so that I would *keep lifting my chin in order to look over it?*" and "I lifted my chin again to see over the wall which rose with me. A kind of soup or stew of all the dungeon stories flew through my head, oubliettes, walls that moved,

---

[5] The first "cell" Camus describes takes on the proportions of a womb, while the second seems to be the birth canal. This metaphorical approach may apply to Golding's work also, as Sammy's cell takes on the proportions of the family bog, where Ma reigned supreme. And of course both writers are suggesting the Fall of Man, implicitly aware of the doctrine of original sin, which, after all, begins with the first fall, with the child's decanting.

the little ease" and finally "The cell was too small for me to stretch myself out." [6]

Yet with all its literary connections, Sammy's cell is his own, private in every sense of the word. (He protects "my privates, our privates, the whole race.") The scene returns to the privy setting of his childhood. The cell, it turns out finally, is a water closet of sorts. The wet, slimy element that Sammy traces out loathingly with his hand, though seemingly a dismemberment, the left-behind penis of some poor body, is only a portion of a damp mop left in a closet used for mops and brooms. Within the darkness of this closet every form of self-torture is visited upon Sammy. But he emerges from the cell with some portion of victory.

Before this emergence can be effected, Golding has several technical difficulties to overcome. One is to show Sammy after World War II, back in England, visiting the asylum in which Beatrice Ifor is now an inmate. With the help of a time shift he arranges one of the most powerful scenes in the entire novel. Sammy is shown within the asylum in the company of a young psychiatrist, Dr. Enticott (a figure who shows how quickly and realistically Golding can integrate a minor character within a plot and make real use of him). Enticott is a friend of Sammy's; they both live on Paradise Hill; and he is more than half in love with Sammy's wife, Taffy. During the period of Sammy's visitation, he makes known this love, and at the same time holds out neither blame nor solace when he discovers Sammy's part in Beatrice's life.

The scene of real power occurs when Beatrice is ushered into the visiting room. Her hair is cut short like a boy's; she makes noises like a bird; her flesh has coarsened; her body is

[6] Italics added.

of a piece, from shoulder to hip the same thickness. When the nurse tries to make her turn to meet Sammy, she jerks round the other way "like the figure in a cathedral clock . . . jerk by jerk through ninety degrees." The rest of the scene unfolds like a bad dream in the daylight:

Beatrice was beginning to stand up. Her hands were clasped into each other. Her mouth was open and her eyes were nittering at me through my tears and sweat.

"That's a good girl!" [the nurse says]

Beatrice pissed over her skirt and her legs and her shoes and my shoes. The pool splashed and spread.

"Miss Ifor dear, naughty—ah, naughty!"

Someone had me by the arm and shoulder and was turning me.

"I think——"

Someone was leading and helping me over acres of bare floor. Marsh-birds were sweeping and crying.

There is no forgiveness from Dr. Enticott or from Beatrice for Sammy. None is possible. To this extent, we are still within the region of Jean Baptiste Clamence's lack of clemency. But the last page of the novel frees us from the region and his indictment, for here we find that his equivalent in Golding's novel, Dr. Halde, has failed with Sammy, as suddenly the cell door is swung open. Left in the cell, Sammy has finally made use of man's last resource, prayer. It is all concentrated in his cry of "Help me! Help me!"—a cry which Pincher stubbornly refuses to make. In this moment Sammy has spiritually burst open the door, having left behind him the shattered crust of the self and selfishness. It remains for the commandant of the camp to actually open the door; he urges Sammy to come out and in so doing apologizes for the treatment Sammy has received at the hands of Dr. Halde. At this moment the commandant is transfigured into one of the Kings of Egypt in

Sammy's eyes. And it is the commandant's words that not only end the novel, but also explain Dr. Halde to Sammy: "The Herr Doctor does not know about peoples." The syntax is wrong but the sympathy is right.

The camp commandant's humane words also provide an answer to Jean Baptiste's contention that everyone is guilty and that forgiveness is impossible. At the novel's end, as in the beginning, Sammy is not someone entirely forgiven and saved; he is, as the first paragraph has it, "a burning amateur." But with his anguished, selfless cry he has purchased release from hell's anteroom, and gained, if not "Paradise Hill," at least a purgatorial stay. He has felt a "pentecostal flame" after his own partial resurrection. We leave him still searching for a way out, with the question of "Here?" still receiving the almost inevitable answer—"Not here," or at least "Not yet."

The comparative elements in the Golding and Camus novels move together—not only the first-person-singular point of view, the confessional tone, the dramatic-monologue technique, but the central question of free will and man's fall, the delayed answer as to where each of the protagonists fell, the connection of each fall with that of a woman, the utilization of highly connotative Biblical names, the concept of rising or mounting to heights as well as joy, the symbolic use of water, the incorporation of "burning bushes," the reference to royalty, the Dantesque and Eliot-like touches, the prison scenes, and the vital question of forgiveness.

Yet with all these elements in common the English book and the French are quite dissimilar in certain important respects. Golding's reactive art arises here not in opposition to Camus so much as to Jean Baptiste Clamence (who should no more be mistaken for Camus than should Sammy Mountjoy for Golding). In this instance, it is as though one of Jean

Baptiste's auditors had answered in his own right—and the answer is "Not that way, but this." In Golding's mind, Jean Baptiste "does not know about peoples," or their relationship with the universe. Golding reverses one of the basic existential tenets: man's position in the universe is not absurd; the universe itself is not; but man's proclivity toward self, toward sin without a concept of atonement, can make him absurd.

The most apparent difference between Golding and Camus leads to all the others: Golding is theological in an unorthodox manner; Camus is logically philosophical. *Free Fall* is a novel filled with highly charged metaphors and allegory; it moves through splotches of color arranged in the mind of a protagonist who is a painter now concerned with presenting a holy picture, replete with pentecostal flames and burning bushes. *The Fall* is lighter, or drier, in tone—witty, sardonic, satirical, and eventually ironic; the lawyer's tone is maintained; his indictment can be stated in one flash of wit—"A single sentence," Jean Baptiste declares, "will suffice for modern man: he fornicated and read the papers."

A short novelette, *The Fall* is nevertheless an extraordinarily unified dramatic monologue, or *récit*. Although it is broken into four or five sections, no harmful pause occurs. In fact, establishment of the pauses decreases the element of tour de force that might otherwise have intruded. If Jean Baptiste's confession were presented all of a piece, it might have some of that same dramatic awkwardness that results in certain works of Conrad's like *Heart of Darkness* and *Lord Jim*. Jean Baptiste gets up, leaves the bar, walks around the city, and takes leave of his *cher compatriote* on several occasions, for such physical necessities as sleep. In this way Camus achieves an extra dimension of verisimilitude. He is able thus to reveal Jean Baptiste's true character bit by bit—able also to show how the auditor would become more and more intrigued, until finally the trap closes softly, with the words *cher maître*. The auditor has been *mon compatriote* or *très cher* until the very end of the novelette when he is accused indirectly of being Jean Baptiste's master—in sin, the implication is. In this way the reader, too, is drawn excruciatingly close to the confession, until he almost feels compelled, as at some highly charged revival meeting, to shout out his sins before the brethren.

La Chute is a seductive book. It moves with wit and grace and impeccable form. It maintains a banteringly humorous tone of high seriousness. Its irony is superb in respect first to Jean Baptiste (the reverse-spin existentialist), then the auditor and finally the reader, who had thought to go unscathed. The author stands behind the scenes implacably brilliant.

Free Fall, by contrast, is a composition that takes as many technical chances as one can afford this side of *le roman nouveau*. Golding's ability to hold, balance, and juggle scenes so that eventually they come down in place is extraordinary. One cannot imagine how those reviewers who called the book unnecessarily complicated ever read Joyce, Gide, or Fenimore Cooper. Golding attempts to hold his narrative construction in as delicate balance as that achieved by his master builder in *The Spire*, sometimes reaching the level of "meta-language"— as exemplified in Sammy's drawing of Beatrice, his immersion in the musky sweetness of the woodland, his sweating horror in prison, and his own physical debasement under Beatrice Ifor's polluted stream. The wonder of Golding's fictive construct is not that it leans a bit this way or that (which it does), or that it sways under pressure (which it also does), but, rather, that it has gone so high—probably high enough to be fairly compared with Camus's classic structure. Placed side by side they present a double vision of man's fall in modern terms.

6

THE NOVEL AS METAPHOR:

THE SPIRE

Heaven abhors the zeal that passes measure.
  —*Euripides*

For me, I think I speak as I was taught.
  —*Browning's painter in "Fra Lippo Lippi"*

WITHIN DAYS after the novel's publication, critics ranging in background from architecture to literature had put on record their findings that Golding's *The Spire* (1964) was a fictional representation of the building of the spire of the cathedral at Salisbury in the fourteenth century. This edifice was one of the great construction feats of the Middle Ages, a fact now belied by its placid, soaring beauty, and the four-hundred-and-four-foot thrust of its graceful spire. Golding's novel has clearly moved the architectural jewel of his home city out of the guidebooks and into literature. Like Golding's master builder, the fourteenth-century architect faced the problem of supporting his four-hundred-foot superstructure on a base of cathedral walls which themselves had only a century-old foundation five feet deep—no more than that of a twentieth-century one-family dwelling. There were only four slim columns to support the spire, and the ground beneath was a marshy meadow skirted by several rivers. Nevertheless, the medieval master builder followed his orders and went ahead, not knowing that beneath the groping plumb lines, probes, and pits the marsh concealed one of the finest weight-bearing geological formations in the world.

According to one tradition, the first bishop of the Salisbury Cathedral chose, after the Virgin appeared to him with appropriate instructions in a vision, a soggy meadow as the site for the construction; while Golding's Dean Jocelin receives the inspiration for his spire in a vision from God. Each edifice is dedicated as the Cathedral Church of the Virgin Mary. Moreover, if a diagram were pieced together from the unobtrusively organized descriptive materials in the novel, it would closely overlay a plan of the Salisbury Cathedral, from Lady Chapel to nave.

The "Barchester"[1] cathedral of Golding's visionary and obsessed Dean Jocelin, like the cathedral at Salisbury, has a spire surmounted by a capstone and a cross, and, to conserve weight, has a skin of ascendingly diminishing thickness. Like Salisbury, iron bands encircle the octagonal tower to strengthen it; and, like Salisbury, the four stone pillars settle and bend, slipping the spire twenty-three inches out of its true perpendicular. The columns that sing in overstrained agony, the stones which storms send down in showers, the ruthlessness with which the construction is forced through to the end, are

---

[1] Anthony Trollope's "Barchester" series of novels admittedly used the geography of Salisbury.

all part of the story of the actual Salisbury as well as of Golding's fiction; but in the novel the spire is also a magnificent symbol which accretes meanings as it thrusts itself upward.

As major symbol, Golding dares to use one which, if the novelist should falter, leaves only a pretentious cliché, for the tower that arises out of a monomaniac obsession has a long tradition; and since the one pressed to completion by Golding's Dean Jocelin is not the first so inspired to make the transition from myth or history into literature, it is inevitable that critics will point to analogues ranging from the Bible's Tower of Babel to "The Bell-Tower" of Melville's Bannadonna, the arrogant and prideful architect whose creation kills him. Readers may also sense the impact of T. S. Eliot's church-building pageant play *The Rock* upon Golding, who is much influenced by Eliot in other ways as well. In *The Rock* attention is focused upon a group of vulgar workmen who are constructing the foundations of a church, indifferent to the task except as it rewards their physical needs. Only Ethelbert, the foreman, is alive to its significance. "There's somethin' strong and lastin' about a buildin'. You needn't believe in God but you've got to believe in a buildin'. It goes up and up in the sky, and on and on through the years . . . and it stands when you and I are dust, what built it for the glory of God—and that church 'as been put up with 'ands, buildin', buildin', buildin'—all through the years—in the ruddy rain and 'eat and 'ail and snow—workin' in bricks and mortar, goin' on forever and ever and ever, buildin' the Church of God." [2]

"The building is a diagram of prayer," Jocelin has told his master builder; "and our spire will be a diagram of the highest

---

[2] Quoted by D. E. Jones in *The Plays of T. S. Eliot* (Toronto, 1960), p. 40.

prayer of all. God revealed it to me in a vision, his unprofitable servant. He chose me. He chooses you, to fill the diagram with glass and iron and stone, since the children of men require a thing to look at. D'you think you can escape?"

To Eliot and to Golding the cost of the Visible Church, the concretizing of man's vision of the infinite, comes high. As Eliot writes in *The Rock:*

> For the work of creation is never without travail;
> The formed stone, the visible crucifix,
> The dressed altar, the lifting light,
>
> Light
>
> Light
>
> The visible reminder of Invisible Light.

Dean Jocelin of Golding's novel is obsessed with the belief that it is his divine mission to raise a glorious tower and spire above his church. His clerical colleagues protest in vain that the project is too expensive, and the edifice unsuited for such a shaft. Jocelin's aptly named master builder, Roger Mason, calculates that the foundations and pillars of the church are inadequate to support the added weight of a four-hundred-foot spire, and fruitlessly tries compromise after compromise to limit the shaft to a less dizzy height. The townspeople—amoral, skeptical, and often literally pagan—are derisive about "Jocelin's Folly." But Jocelin forces the work onward more by his "blazing will" than by his piety. He has visions in which an angel—whose hot presence he often feels behind him—urges him on. He obtains tainted money from his worldly aunt, Lady Alison, a favorite of the King, who had once used her charms to obtain, among other things, Jocelin's rapid promotion in the Church—a rise the Dean naïvely thought had come through divine call, rather than postcoital royal whim. He blackmails Mason and his army of builders to proceed with the construction by making it impossible for him and his band of architectural mercenaries to get work elsewhere. Yet Mason, who opposes each stage of the enterprise, knowing that his professional reputation as well as his freedom as a human being are becoming as undermined as the cathedral's foundations, reluctantly goes on with the work, and the spire rises.

The foundations shudder; the pillars sing under their increasing burden; the chaos in the church brings an end to all worship within; the chaos outside alienates Jocelin from the chapter as well as from the community; while the builder's unruly mercenaries drink, fornicate, murder, and brawl away their leisure hours; but the work goes on. Jocelin neglects all his spiritual duties to be up in the tower overseeing the workmen himself, all the while choosing not to see within and without himself what might interrupt the spire's dizzying climb. The physical and emotional wreckage increases along with Jocelin's monomania, as pride, stubbornness, and self-delusion only accelerate his relentlessness. "The folly isn't mine," he tells himself. "It's God's Folly." (But the statement is complicated by our realization that *Jocelin* can mean *fool*.) The folly has its cost, wherever the guilt lies, and the price includes the beautiful, flaming-haired Goody Pangall, miserably married to a sickly, impotent cathedral caretaker. She becomes mistress to Mason; and Jocelin, aware of the relationship, chooses to ignore it lest it cost him his foreman's services. Yet the Dean himself cannot suppress the true nature of his own sensual feelings for Goodwife Pangall—his "daughter in God"—whom he had known in preconstruction days as a shy, demure girl whose presence around the cloisters he enjoyed. At more than one point he becomes acutely aware of her red hair and white flesh, but deludes himself into thinking there is nothing wrong. He cannot understand that his crises of body and soul have their parallels in the crises and tragedies which accompany the rising of the shaft.

When the cathedral's foundations are excavated at one place to determine how much weight they can bear, foul odors erupt from the pit, a figurative hell mouth. It is clear that they contain at least one putrescent corpse; and in the frenzy of his obsession, evil impulses well up from the "cellarage" (a *Pincher Martin* symbol as well) of Jocelin's mind. "There is no innocent work," he muses. "God knows where God may be." And the stones rise into the sky, although only Jocelin believes that they will remain there. The spire continues to stand despite a violent storm which damages it. But Jocelin disintegrates, tormented by a crippling disease which wrecks his spine, and by erotic visions of Goody Pangall (who dies in childbirth, while Jocelin foolishly tries to intervene). He begins to suspect that his "angel" may have been a devil in disguise, and that he has really fallen under the spell of Goody's "witchcraft." Devils and angels now visit him one after the other; still, he can find paradoxical satisfaction, as he lies dying, that the spire is finished, topped with a Holy Nail. Imperfectly realized as it is, it is nevertheless Jocelin's envisioned spire of prayer. In his hubris it is his only prayer, for his last days are spent in bed speechless, under the shadow of the maimed spire, his ears ringing with the curses of the master builder to whom, near the end, he had painfully crept to offer belated and useless amends. The spire does not topple, wrong though it theoretically is for the structure it so precariously graces at the novel's close. Only Jocelin has fallen.

The overheated, nearly choking intensity of Golding's narrative encloses the reader in the hysterical mind of the Dean in the same way that the range of metaphorical treatment of the spire, integral to the theme, evokes the Dean's feverish, oscillating states of mind. The spire, maimed, like his spine, at the close, is successively the mast of a ship, the Ark of God, a "diagram of prayer," the phallus of a supine man, a "dunce's cap," a "stone hammer . . . waiting to strike." Only a relatively short novel can maintain the tension needed to propel such a narrative forward, and Golding's novel, in his typical fashion, is short. Paralysis or mystification—or both—might have resulted from attempting to sustain the mood through additional verbiage.

A second symbol, less pervasive but almost as intriguing as the spire itself, is that of the apple tree. Two lines given to Jocelin are set in italics: *"There is no innocent work. God knows where God may be."* and *"It's like the apple tree!"* The novel's development explains the first statement—and is practically its gloss. The second is gnomic and puzzling, until we recall that Jocelin had understood that the concretizing of his vision was likely to have complex repercussions; for not only is there no innocent work, but simplicity is also a deception: "A single green shoot at first, then clinging tendrils, then branches. . . ." Later Jocelin goes out into the brilliant spring sunshine and sees an apple tree in full blossom:

There was a cloud of angels flashing in the sunlight, they were pink and gold and white; and they were uttering this sweet scent for joy of the light and the air. They brought with them a scatter of clear leaves, and among the leaves a long, black springing thing. His head swam with the angels, and suddenly he understood there was more to the apple tree than one branch. It was there beyond the wall, bursting up with cloud and scatter, laying hold of the earth and the air, a fountain, a marvel, an apple tree; and this made him weep in a childish way so that he could not tell whether he was glad or sorry.

"It's like the apple tree" seems primarily a reference to the fact that the great spire, like the trunk of a tree, thrusts grandly upward, but also thrusts in many other directions, many—like the mixed nature of man's motives and works—too complex to be seen at first view. Yet it also seems inescapable that Golding has chosen an apple tree rather than any other because it is his intention to remind us of that most notorious of apple trees, whose fruit precipitated man's expulsion from Eden. Again Golding has found it impossible to evade the most obsessive subject in his fiction, the Fall.

The conflict between the Dean and his architect creates one of the basic tensions of the novel, the basic one outside Jocelin himself. Spiritually, Jocelin himself is the master builder, both in conceiving his vision and eventually in driving the project on; while Mason, his craft, and his craftsmen are being used— and victimized—for Jocelin's fanatical purpose. "I will urge him up stone by stone, if I have to," the Dean vows. "He has no vision. He is blind." But Jocelin wants the impossible, and believes that through faith it can be attained, while Mason has only earthly skill and earthy wisdom, and knows that faith, however elevated, cannot raise a satisfactory spire on unstable foundations. "Lord," cries Jocelin, "what instruments we have to use!" Like Pincher Martin and Sammy Mountjoy, he cannot see people as people. To Jocelin they are only instruments of his relentless purpose.

It is difficult not to think of another master builder and his project in connection with Golding's novel, for the term *master builder*—pervasive in the novel—is the title itself of one of the great plays in the modern repertory, Ibsen's *The Master Builder* (1892). Shortly before Ibsen conceived his play he had heard the legend of the master builder of Munich, who had built St. Michael's Church there, and had thrown himself down from the tower of the church because he was afraid that he had built too high, and that the roof would collapse under the stresses and strains he had put upon it. Ibsen said that he thought the legend must have arisen in Scandinavia, and when others observed that every famous cathedral in Germany had the same legend in some variation, Ibsen replied that it must have arisen from the popular feeling that man could not build so high without paying the penalty for his hubris.[3]

Ibsen's Master Builder is Solness, a specialist in erecting churches, a man who habitually and arrogantly uses other people to achieve his purposes, in particular a young employee, Ragnar Brovik, whose architectural skills are superior to his own. The major construction project of the play is a high tower Solness insists on building as an appendage to his own new house—a bizarre and unnecessary feature. He had vowed not to build any more churches, and intends the spire either to somehow counteract the force of his vow or to be the concrete symbol of the mystical powers he believes he has. The tower becomes the focus of his monomania, the result of his feeling that God has singled him out as a builder of churches for His glory. But he feels, more than half in earnest, that he is being driven on by devils or trolls; that in a way they serve him, but by constantly pandering to his evil instincts and desires—both sacrilegious and sexual—they have come to be the rulers of his will, mysterious powers which make him

[3] Michael Meyer, notes to his translation of *The Master Builder*, in *When We Dead Awaken* (New York, 1960), pp. 128–29. Quotations from *The Master Builder* are also from this edition.

afraid of himself, make him afraid to look into his motives. "But please God," cries Ibsen's spire-builder, "I may never become a troll like the one who mocks me in everything I do! Everything!" When asked what he means, he adds, "Everything I have created . . . I must sit here and expiate! Pay for it. Not with money. But with human happiness. . . . And not only with my happiness, but with the happiness of others, too." Solness also worries about the nature of the invisible demons he senses about him, tempting and driving him. "Good demons and evil demons," he muses. "Fair demons and dark. If only one always knew whether it was the fair that had hold of one or the dark!"

Jocelin's angel appears—so he first thinks—to strengthen and warm him. Soon his angel becomes merged in his consciousness with Satan, who torments his dreams, so that the stones of the tower become "hot to his feet with all the fires of hell." Toward the end he feels "his angel and his devil at war behind his back." (The warmth at his back turns out to be the incipient disease which kills him, tuberculosis of the spine.)

"I am bewitched," Jocelin cries. And he is. But he has no idea at first that he is as much bewitched by his repressed manliness as by his expressed godliness. Solness is similarly bewitched, and again by a beautiful young woman he had known since her girlhood days. Hilde Wangel is a far shrewder female, however, than Goody Pangall, and not at all the passive creature custom decreed proper for the medieval goodwife. But both young women have an irresistible sexual charm, and the action of *The Master Builder* is concerned with the effect of Hilde's presence upon Solness, as he more and more succumbs to her impetuous will, and his obsession with his spire becomes more and more the phallic sublimation of his feelings for her. She demands that he do "the impossible" by climbing the completed tower to accomplish the topping ritual himself. It *is* "the impossible" because Solness has developed a morbid fear of heights even severer than the sudden vertigo Jocelin experiences each time he drives himself to the top of his spire. To see the Master Builder mount the tower, and wreathe the spire, is the fulfillment of all the sexually arrested Hilde has craved, and her vicarious ecstasy as he fearfully accomplishes the feat sends her into orgasm—apparently the only way she can reach such a climax. The tower survives the ceremony, but the Master Builder does not, falling to his death as his over-strained nerves snap. There is a wild singing from the top of the spire, called by some the wind in the trees, and by Hilde harps in the air; and the Master Builder's body plunges into the stone pit at the side of the building, at the base of the shaft.

To his astonishment, Jocelin discovers that his master builder fears heights even more than he does. He fears them but endures them as part of his craft, while Jocelin savors his vertigo symptoms, enjoying the "breath-catching exultation of a quivering plank . . . over a sheer drop." In a way it is the pleasure Ibsen's Hilde feels vicariously at the spire-topping. The wreathing of the spire, a propitiation of the gods, has its equivalent in Jocelin's setting of the Holy Nail into the top of his cathedral's spire. He takes the Nail, in a silver box on the altar, and climbs up the swaying shaft though suffering his worst spasms of vertigo. His heart hits him at the base of his throat as he begins to climb the corkscrew stairs; lights dance about him in the blackness, and the spire's screaming assails him; and he ascends trembling "like a man climbing a mast at sea." At the top he beats the Nail into the wood with the soft silver box. The vertigo gets almost uncontrollable, but—unlike Ibsen's Solness—he manages to descend safely. But by the time he retraces his steps to the corkscrew stairs, he is crawling. Outside he senses "a wave of ineffable good sweetness, wave after wave, and an atonement."

At the opening of Ibsen's play Solness had been seen suppressing with difficulty his jealous desire for Kaja, a young secretary betrothed to his chief architect, whose will he dominates easily. Solness's wife, the listless, brooding Aline, broken by past personal tragedies and sunk in her religious devotions, accepts all that happens as the visitations of heaven, and part of Solness's nagging sense of guilt has been his feeling of never having devoted himself sufficiently to her. His new dwelling—with spire—was to be for her, and for his expiation.

The cathedral is Jocelin's bible in stone, and the spire his prayer rising from it. His preoccupation with the spire is also the phallic sublimation of his long-repressed yearnings for the red-haired young Goody Pangall, a yearning which becomes more obsessive as he jealously watches her drift into a liaison with the Dean's architect, Roger Mason. In Jocelin's visions, Satan has her blazing hair—and sometimes her garments—and after her death she continues to urge him on, agonizing him with the witchcraft of his burning memory of her flesh and hair. He identifies utterly with his building—his body—and with the spire, an erect phallus, and when Satan torments him he is seized "by the loins, so that it became indeed an unruly member," justifying Golding's having once toyed half-seriously with the idea of titling his novel *An Erection in Barchester*. To construct the glorious erection that is the spire itself, Jocelin must endure the befoulment of the edifice, defiled by obscene, godless workmen who sometimes even desert the job to indulge in pagan rites. And the price of Jocelin's manifold glory is his discovery of his not-unwilling befoulment.

With typical Golding double vision the church is not only a body Jocelin sees, but Jocelin's own body as well. The edifice

which is his "diagram of prayer" is (in a model before him)
also

like a man lying on his back. The nave was his legs placed together, the transepts on either side were his arms outspread. The
choir was his body; and the Lady Chapel . . . was his head. And
now also, springing, projecting, bursting, erupting from the heart
of the building, there was its crown and majesty, the new spire.

But we are not sure how accurate Jocelin's vision is, whether
the spire arises from God's heart, or loins, and we discover in
moments of the Dean's self-condemnation that he has what
the cathedral itself lacks, for he thinks of himself as "a building
with a vast cellarage" (recalling for us *Pincher Martin*) as well
as a building with a spire. The workmen desecrate his vision
by holding the model of the spire obscenely between their legs,
and Jocelin—in his bed—imagines that

he was lying on his back in the marshes, crucified, and his arms
were the transepts. . . . Only Satan himself, rising out of the west,
clad in nothing but blazing hair stood over his nave and worked
at the building, tormenting him so that he writhed on the marsh
in the warm water, and cried out aloud. He woke in the darkness,
full of loathing.

To the end he is uncertain whether he has been inspired by
a true vision, by worldly vanity, or by witchcraft of the flesh.
He has his doubts but the compulsion to drive on is stronger
than any inhibitions brought on by thoughts of the consequences. "Out of some deep place," Jocelin tells his foreman,
"comes the command to do what makes no sense at all—to
build a ship on dry land; to sit among the dunghills; to marry
a whore; to set their son on the altar of sacrifice." The vision
made concrete loses a good deal of its glory and has its cruel
human cost. It is beautiful in its simplicity only while it remains

the glorious vision, but it is man's nature to attempt, and to endure, the concretizing of the vision. A shaft on a house of prayer unequal to it, a shaft on a dwelling house unsuited for it—the obsessive vision is as beyond logic as it is, for the aspirer, beyond question.

Much of *The Spire* seems a reactive impulse from Ibsen,[4] the playwright whose major theme was (in Shaw's words) "the power of ideals to kill," the power of ideals to delude us as to our true motives, and their complexity of cross-purposes. The spire susceptible to Freudian glosses, the young man involved in the obsession over the spire, the vertigo symptoms of both master builders (as well as Jocelin), the Christian-pagan symbolism of the topping rituals, the visitations by angels and devils, the wholesale ruin of lives and careers by forceful men who see other human beings only as their instruments: these, and other elements touched upon earlier, relate the spires of Ibsen and Golding. And coincidentally, in the light of the cathedral setting of Golding's novel, *The Master Builder* has been called "a great cathedral of a play."[5]

There is still another Ibsen drama of which theme and title character demand consideration with respect to *The Spire:* the verse tragedy *Brand* (1866). Brand, the minister of God, is an idealist of obsessive, uncompromising earnestness. No one and nothing is spared in his demonic zeal to have everyone live—on his terms—a saintly life. His will is unconquerable. He never falters, even when his own small son, like Abraham's, must be sacrificed to the Lord. Neither is his wife spared, nor his mother. Possessed by his demon, he goes ahead pitilessly to build the great new church he has envisioned. (The soul can-

---

[4] The Michael Meyer translations of *Brand* and *Master Builder* were published to widely favorable notices in 1960.
[5] Robert Brustein, *The Theatre of Revolt* (New York: 1964), p. 77.

not rise in the old church, he complains.) As the spire climbs upward, the people of the Norse village that Brand serves grow uneasy that retribution must follow such single-minded frenzy. The great church, completed, brings no peace to Brand, who can find nothing to admire:

> "I shall rebuild the Lord's house and make it greater"—
> That was my boast. Is this what I had envisaged?
> Is this the vision I once had
> Of a vault spanning the world's pain?

Brand cannot be happy with a church built by the hands of fallible men who live like beasts and are lost in a thousand daily compromises which undermine their integrity. For him it is all or nothing. Only when the villagers destroy everything that is rotten within themselves can they build the great cathedral which would be one with the Word of God. He leads his flock up into the ice-choked mountains to find God's true church, one not built with hands at all, the Ice Church of folk legend and the embodiment of his obsessive imagination. The people desert him, but in his fanaticism he goes on, soon accompanied by a seductive and unearthly female figure reminiscent of his dead wife, and then by another, and younger, female, also out of his past. At the mountain chasm called the Ice Church, where "cataract and avalanche sing Mass," and a forbidding black peak is church spire, an avalanche roars down upon Brand. He has found his church, but must cry out hopelessly,

> Answer me, God, in the moment of death!
> If not by Will, how can Man be redeemed? [6]

---

[6] The translations from *Brand* are from the translation by Michael Meyer (New York, 1960).

Still, like Jocelin, the shattered Brand has achieved a moral victory, albeit through the sacrifice of everything he loved in the world—as Shaw put it in *The Quintessence of Ibsenism*, through "having caused more intense suffering by his saintliness than the most talented sinner could possibly have done with twice his opportunities." The Ibsen dramas and Golding's fiction both end with the spire-topped edifices dominating their human progenitors, and the villain-idealist protagonists dead.

Golding, in reusing in his fashion the myths Ibsen dramatized, and in applying them to the fact of the Salisbury spire, has given his own moral and imaginative shape to them. He has also invested his novel with a complexity and a density beyond allegory, which, from many levels, and with his unique distinction of style, aspires to give—among other preoccupations—Golding's own answers to Ibsen's speculations: the questionable innocence of faith, the subterranean ramifications of a vision, the dubious heroism of a zeal that passes measure, the paradox of a love that corrupts and destroys. Critics and commentators are often beguiled by their own theses, and may attempt to make too much of their findings. Certainly *The Spire* is less literarily reactive than Golding's earlier novels, even when we consider the ancestry of other elements in the novel not yet examined. For without Golding's seventeen years as a master in Bishop Wordsworth's School, under the shadow of the great spire in Salisbury, and that spire's carefully recorded and preserved chronicles, there would be no novel, powerfully as Golding seems to have been affected by Ibsen. Nevertheless, it is no small achievement that Golding's fictional edifice—although a deeply personal expression—bears comparison with Ibsen.

———

Throughout the charged atmosphere of *The Spire*, the reader may be seized by the haunting sensation of familiar people, places, and things. It may not only be that the setting is a familiar one to literature, but that Golding's reading in Browning lurks beneath the novel's surface—particularly the dramatic monologue "The Bishop Orders His Tomb at Saint Praxed's Church" (1845).[7] Browning's Renaissance bishop, immobilized upon his deathbed—a pallet in the church itself—lingers over his memories, such savory recollections as his passion for a fair young woman, his rivalry with a fellow cleric, and is attended at his deathbed by a character named Anselm. Golding's Jocelin loathes his rival ecclesiastic Anselm (his confessor), and has a scarcely concealed passion for his sexton's wife. Browning's bishop recalls stealing and hiding a precious stone from a burning church, and wants to take it with him into eternity. "So, let the blue lump poise between my knees," he tells his "nephews." The image seems to reappear in *The Spire*, when Dean Jocelin watches a dumb stonecutter in a leather apron, "the lump of stone between his knees."

There are apparent echoes of Browning's diction, his "blessed mutter of the mass" appearing in *The Spire* as "a hoarse and private mutter," and later as "a mutter of mass priests." At the end, both priests are obsessed by thoughts that they have fallen through vanity, and by the consequences and new needs that oncoming death requires. Like Browning's bishop, Jocelin wants a proper sarcophagus, and familiar images arise:

---

[7] Ian Gregor ("Aspiring," *Manchester Guardian Weekly*, April 16, 1964, p. 11), discussing the increasingly complex meanings Golding's narratives take, and the strain put upon them by this burden, concludes: "In this way *The Spire* is reminiscent of Browning's dramatic monologues in its elliptical form, its introspective intensity, its risking a larger freight than it can safely carry." But he proceeds no further.

At one point he began to think about his tomb and managed to send for the dumb man. Through an interminable succession of time and gap he got him to understand what was wanted; himself without ornament, lying stripped in death of clothing and flesh, a prone skeleton lapped in skin, head fallen back, mouth open. He plucked at the bedclothes, and at last hands understood. They stripped him for the young man, who drew with a face of fascinated disgust while Jocelin drifted away again. After a century or two the young man had gone, and a fly cleaned its legs on the vaulting.

Once there were candles, voices murmuring, and the touch of oil. He floated above the unction which had relevance to nothing but the leaden body. . . .

So, too, Browning's bishop lies on a pallet in the church, staring at the vaulting, plucking at his bedclothes. "Dying by degrees," he plans the details of his tomb and his carved effigy, and dreams of feeling eternally "the steady candle-flame" and incense smoke, while the voices of his ungrieving heirs murmur about his bed and he senses through his intermittent delirium that his posthumous pilgrimage will not be equal to his earlier hopes.

Not unexpectedly, the lush—yet more economical—texture of *The Spire* recalls Golding's preceding novel, *Free Fall*, although the later novel has, rather than the reverie-like pace of time remembered, the hysterical pitch of nightmare. There is the symbolic obsession with fire, and with sunlight, and the density of imagery in general. And if some of the texture and background of *The Spire* recalls one Browning dramatic monologue, an episode in *Free Fall* recalls another. The evidence appears when, late in the novel, Sammy Mountjoy recalls his days in a "little country grammar school," particularly an episode involving Miss Rowena Pringle, his form

mistress, "a middle-aged spinster with sandy hair and the beginnings of a sandy moustache and beard." Miss Pringle's
religious fanaticism—partly the misdirected reaction of her
fruitless passion for Sammy's guardian, Father Watts-Watt—
takes the form, in Sammy's case, of a belief that his interest in
the Bible is entirely a search for smut. The circumstantial evidence, she believes, is Sammy's rough workbook, and, reluctantly, under her insistence, he exposes the now-coverless book
for scrutiny:

> I began to turn the pages. . . .
> Arithmetic and a horse pulling the roller over the town cricket
> pitch. Some wrongly spelt French verbs, repeated. A cart on the
> weighing machine outside the town hall. . . . Arithmetic, Latin.
> Some profiles. A landscape, not drawn, so much as noted down
> and then elaborated. . . . In the middle distance was a complica-
> tion of trees and hillocks into which the eye was drawn and into
> which the troubled spectator could vanish. . . .

Miss Pringle, still searching for sex and sacrilege, compels an
even more intensive scrutiny, and examines the landscape
"inch by inch" giving "the edge of the rough work book little
taps so that it moved round and presented my hillocks, my
scalloped downs and deep woodlands to her, upright." The
revelation is almost too much, and she shudders with outrage
and condemnation, then—expulsion in mind—turns him over
to the headmaster, with whom she has a whispered, preliminary interview.

Searching for the page which inspired the pious outrage,
the headmaster, too, finally comes upon the landscape and
"plunged through the paper among the hillocks and trees. . . .
Suddenly he did what Miss Pringle had done—turned the book
so that my lovely curved downs were upright, the patch of

intricate woodland projecting from them." His reaction is different, though, his "appalled realization" is clear to Sammy, who sees on the headmaster's face "impotence to cope . . . even the beginning of wild laughter." After a few platitudes about the wrongfulness of using the workbook for drawing, uttered while still leafing through the book, the headmaster's words abruptly cease. He has caught sight of something which had escaped Miss Pringle:

It was a page where I had drawn as many of the form as I could. Some of them had defeated me; but for one or two I had drawn face after face, elaborating then simplifying so that the final result gave me a deep satisfaction as I sent the passionate message down the pencil. He pushed his spectacles up on his forehead and held the page close.

"That's young Spragg!"

At that the chaos came out of my eyes. It was wet and warm and I could not stop.

Although not in Miss Pringle's class, Sammy is left free to pursue his art, and is particularly abetted by another member of the faculty, "Old Nick" Shales, the science teacher. "What I like about your drawings," Shales tells him, "is that they look like the things they're meant to be." Eventually Sammy has the opportunity of an art class, and is astonished by the results of a sketch hastily drawn for someone else:

In carelessness and luck I had put the girl on paper in a way that my laborious portraitures could never come at. The line leapt, it was joyous, free, authoritative. It achieved little miracles of implication so that the viewer's eye created her small hands though my pencil had not touched them. That free line had raced past and created her face. . . .

Eventually Sammy's sacrilege has been transformed into a career in art, in the same fashion as that of Browning's "Fra Lippo Lippi" (1855). The hero of Browning's dramatic monologue, like Sammy Mountjoy, is an orphaned boy taken into custody, fed and trained, by men of the cloth. Where Sammy's guardian is an Anglican minister, and his school a religiously oriented grammar school, Lippo—a Renaissance child—is in the custody of monks, and made a novice as a result; and his school is a Carmelite monastery. But he, too, has the artist's urge, and his notebooks intersperse drawings with the reluctantly learned Latin and sacred music:

> I drew men's faces on my copy-books,
> Scrawled them within the antiphonary's marge
> Joined legs and arms to the long music-notes,
> Found eyes and nose and chin for A's and B's,
> And made a string of pictures of the world
> Betwixt the ins and outs of verb and noun. . . .

Lippo is found out, and the monks who catch him in the act look black, and turn him over to the Prior, for expulsion. Like Sammy's headmaster, the Prior is not so piously outraged, and has other ideas:

> "Nay," quoth the Prior, "turn him out, d'ye say?
> In no wise. . . ."

Lippo is bade to daub away, and he covers the monastery's blank walls, drawing "every sort of monk," little children and even the opposite sex. The monks, having been "taught what to see and not to see," do not at first comprehend the triumphs of Lippo's art:

"That's the very man!
Look at the boy who stoops to pat the dog!
That woman's like the Prior's niece who comes
To care about his asthma: it's the life!"
But there my triumph's straw-fire flared and funked;
Their betters took their turn to see and say:
The Prior and the learned pulled a face
And stopped all that in no time. "How? what's here?
Quite from the mark of painting, bless us all!
Faces, arms, legs, and bodies like the true
As much as pea and pea! it's devil's game. . . .
Give us no more of body than shows soul!"

Lippo manages a career in art anyway; his troubles, like
Sammy's, arise later from fulfilling the desires intensified by
the flesh he paints. Sammy Mountjoy is, certainly, no Lippo
in genius, but in his boyhood confrontations with his own
sensuality, as well as with the adult world's reaction—in a
religious context—to his furtive explorations of his artistic
talent, he is doubtless another example of how Golding has
used his reading in his own art.

7

AMBASSADORS AT LARGE: OTHER WRITINGS

This obsession with writing is as pointless as
alcoholism and there's no Authors Anonymous to
wean you from the typewriter.

> —*William Golding, in "It's a Long Way*
> *to Oxyrhynchus"*

*N*OTWITHSTANDING his admitted obsession with the typewriter, Golding has published a relatively small body of work. Except during a three-year period from 1960 through 1962, when he produced a substantial number of reviews and occasional writings for *The Spectator* (it was, significantly, during his longest gap between published novels), and an earlier period in the fifties, when he accepted several BBC writing assignments, he has written little for publication other than his novels.

In addition to contributing some essays and reviews to periodicals, Golding has produced an early (1934) book of poems, a novella and a full-length play, and two works specifically written for the BBC in the late fifties, *Miss Pulkinhorn*, a radio play with strong religious overtones, and *Break My Heart*, a shorter radio drama.

The novella and play, *Envoy Extraordinary* (1956) and *The Brass Butterfly* (1958) are closely related, for one is a dramatization of the other, first produced under the earlier title as a play for BBC radio, later produced under the new title in an expanded version at the Strand Theatre, London, in 1958 with Alastair Sim in the leading role. The tale is set in the days of Imperial Rome. Phanocles, an Alexandrian Greek inventor-genius, turns up at the court of one of the Caesars, bearing models of three inventions, and the idea for an even more dangerous fourth. All are technologically sound, but (as is the history of many inventions since) produced at the wrong time in the wrong place. With him Phanocles brings, too, his apparently mute (but beautiful) sister, Euphrosyne, who provides the romantic interest when the Emperor's illegitimate—and innocent—grandson, Mamillius, falls in love with her. In addition to the worldly-wise Emperor the only other leading character is the arrogant and suspicious General Postumus, his "Heir Designate"—the "heavy" of the drama.

The long story is simple in plot. Postumus schemes to inherit the empire earlier than he should, and is eventually (and literally) hoist with his own petard. The Emperor proves that the aristocratic humanist can inherit the earth. And Phanocles learns what all inventor-geniuses learn—that the world is never ready to undergo any violent change, even for the better, and his technological revolution is aborted.

The first invention, that of a ship propelled by steam, interests the Emperor sufficiently to make him order a full-sized prototype constructed, but General Postumus fears it and has the *Amphitrite* sabotaged and burned. The second invention, gunpowder, is held in check (temporarily) by the brass butterfly—the firing pin on Phanocles's cannon. The third interests the Emperor more than the others, and is an outgrowth of the use of steam for driving power. "The most Promethean discovery of them all," the Emperor gloats as he savors a trout prepared in Phanocles's pressure cooker. Disappointed, the inventor voices his hope that great inventions will be better received in that future "when men are free because they no longer believe themselves to be slaves—" The Emperor (in the novella) shakes his head in disagreement:

"You work among perfect elements and therefore politically you are an idealist. There will always be slaves though the name may change. What is slavery but the domination of the weak by the strong? How can you make them equal? Or are you fool enough to think that men are born equal? . . . As for your explosive—it has preserved me this day and therefore the peace of the Empire. But it has cost the Empire a merciless ruler who would have murdered half a dozen people and given justice to a hundred million. The world has lost a bargain. No, Phanocles. We will restore Jove's own bolt to his random and ineluctible hand."

It is Phanocles's last opportunity to seek royal sponsorship for his major technological feats, and he draws from his belt a sample of the work of an invention he has dramatically held in reserve—a method of multiplying books he calls "printing." At first the novella's Emperor is ecstatically enthusiastic. Then he has second thoughts. There might not be enough genius to go round. The world might be glutted with trivia and trash: "I built Hadrian's Wall"; "The Unconscious Symbolism of the first book of Euclid"; "I was Nero's Grandmother"; "Metrical Innovations in the Mimes of Herondas." The Emperor's terror grows. "Military, Naval, Sanitary, Eugenic—I shall have to read them all! Political, Statistical, Medical—"

He changes the subject back to Phanocles's Imperial reward, and offers the inventor an ambassadorship, an appointment beyond the dreams of the lowborn, and one which connects Phanocles's inventions to actual history. "You can take your explosive and your printing with you. I shall make you Envoy Extraordinary and Plenipotentiary. . . . Phanocles, my dear friend. I want you to go to China." When Golding dramatized the tale as *The Brass Butterfly* he altered the last speech to take advantage of a line from a once-popular expression, later incorporated into a once-popular song: "Phanocles, my dear friend—I want you to take a *slow* boat to China."

There are far more substantial changes which accompany the transition from tale to comedy. While the dialogue in the novella has the ornate, metaphor-laden quality of a Christopher Fry play, Golding's comedy retains only the more colloquial, speakable lines, and sharpens the tone of the reworked dialogue, producing lines with Shavian crispness, Shavian paradoxes, and Shavian anachronistic wit. Few of the elaborate descriptive passages from the story survive, and then only as stage directions. The construction of the paddle-wheeled *Amphitrite*—from an old corn barge—appears only in the novella (apparently dropped as unstageable); and the sentimental scene in which, early in the story, Mamillius asks Phanocles for his sister's hand, is only intimated in the play. Instead Golding writes in a confrontation between Mamillius and a more glamorous (than in the novella) Euphrosyne, a scene with greater dramatic possibilities, as well as one which enlarges the role of the sole female character (who, in the novella had, antiromantically, turned out to have a harelip—a blemish removed in the play version). Postumus, too, is given an enlarged role, while Mamillius, somewhat diminished, is less the figure of fun, his idealism losing several degrees of its ridiculousness. And Phanocles's single-minded devotion to Reason and Progress is intensified beyond satire into broad caricature.

In setting and dialogue, the beginning and the end of *The Brass Butterfly* follow the novella closely. The body of the play is the most changed, partly out of exigencies of the stage, partly to give the characters more credibility. But the basic ideas remain unaltered. Improved technology does not improve humanity, the Emperor understands. The enthusiastic Phanocles sees no limits to what man can do with his universe, but cannot comprehend the danger of playing Prometheus to unready, unwilling man. "You were going to change the universe," says the Emperor. "Will you improve it?" It is a theme which harks back to the novels, particularly *Lord of the Flies* and *The Inheritors*, where Golding sees progress as a bag of mixed blessings. The most suggestive working-out of the Prometheus myth is clearly in *Pincher Martin*, but in other novels as well, man the bringer of knowledge must suffer for his efforts, which are "hubristic" (as the Emperor tells Phanocles) as well as altruistic. In *Lord of the Flies*, Piggy has literally (through his glasses) taken fire from heaven. In *The Inheritors* the bringers of new knowledge are—in the mass—bringers of additional sin and guilt. In *The Spire* Dean Jocelin recalls the Edenic apple tree. "Phanocles," the Emperor confides in the play, "in my experience changes have seldom been for the better, since the universe does not seem to give something for nothing." Much of this mood is in the play, but not in the more superficial earlier story, which aimed for its effects through nothing stronger than wryness.

The play has some of the qualities of a Shaw play of the

Caesar and Cleopatra type—arch wit, deliberate anachronism, sardonic tone, Roman Empire setting. And there are echoes of *Androcles and the Lion* as well, in the seeming parody of the Lavinia–Roman Captain relationship through the romance of Golding's Mamillius and Euphrosyne:

Euphrosyne. I have nothing to give in exchange.
Mamillius. Yourself!
Euphrosyne. I had nothing but my God. . . .
Mamillius. I will share your gods!
Euphrosyne. If only you could!
Mamillius. If you believe, that is enough for me. Your gods shall be my gods!
Euphrosyne. My *God* shall be thy God.
Mamillius. Very well. Thy *God* shall be my God. Kiss me.
  (*They embrace.*)

Although the plot is reminiscent of "The Rewards of Industry," a story in Richard Garnett's *Twilight of the Gods* (1888), the Mamillius–Euphrosyne relationship in the play is clearly a vehicle for an unorthodox approach to Christianity, almost in the Shavian manner. Again the dialogue is an addition to the far more superficial *Envoy Extraordinary* tale, which serves as scenario for most of the play. When the firing pin—the Brass Butterfly of Phanocles's cannon—is removed by Euphrosyne, there is an explosion, miraculous to all but the rationalistic inventor, and the enemy is destroyed. Sensing a divine visitation, Mamillius forgets, in his excitement, his recent conversion:

Mamillius. Euphrosyne, my love—we are saved! Jupiter has destroyed our enemies!
Euphrosyne. It was our God! He guided my hand—
Mamillius (incredulous). The God of Love?—Striking people with lightning?

Euphrosyne. But He is the God of Battles, too! . . .

Mamillius (triumphant). Abandon Jupiter, Grandfather! Grandfather—did you hear? Love and War at one altar! This is com-
prehensive!

The Emperor, of course, interprets the incident in his own
religious terms, rejecting both Christian explanations and
Phanocles's talk of Law and Change and Reason. And this
scene can only inspire speculation as to how orthodox a
Christian view Golding really represents.

In the play Golding also employs the Shavian technique of
paradox, particularly in approaching the past unawed and in
letting it speak in terms of the present. In Shaw's *Caesar and
Cleopatra* we have a deliberately anachronistic steam engine
servicing an Alexandrian lighthouse. In *The Brass Butterfly*
we have the technologist's steamship, which gets a cold initial
reception from the Emperor:

Emperor. You will say I am old—but I prefer a slow boat. We will
have nothing but slow boats in the future.

Phanocles. But Caesar!

Emperor. Besides, have you considered how unfair she was to the
slaves?

Phanocles. She would have made them unnecessary.

Emperor. Well, there you are, you see. To be a slave-rower is a
hard life, Phanocles, but it is better than no life at all. You do
not have to think of these things, but I am responsible for the
well-being of all classes. Your fast boats would lead to nothing
but a pool of unemployment, and I am not hardhearted enough
to countenance that.

More perceptive than the brilliant Phanocles, Golding's Emperor understands the difference between progress and change,
and sees little chance, given man's unchanging nature, that
man will ever learn to use his intelligence any more wisely or

well merely because he has increased the number and complexity of his tools. Automation, the Emperor reasons, is a serious problem, even though life truly "was not organized to make men happy."

In a review, a few years later, Golding observed in what is almost a gloss upon *The Brass Butterfly* and the novels that when we look down upon the history of man from the height of archaeological findings, "we can see the sack of Babylon and the blasting of Hiroshima as one and the same thing, a disease endemic but not incurable. It is not too much to say that man invented war at the very earliest moment possible. It is not too much to say that as soon as he could leave an interpretable sign of anything, he left a sign of his belief in God. . . . Knowledge of his tragic past should render him less of a slave to the future." [1] Although Shaw's faith in Creative Evolution (which waned somewhat as he lived on into World War II and the Atomic Age) was based upon the sense that the world could and would have to be remade eventually by better and wiser men, his meliorism, even early in his career, was scarcely any more guarded than Golding's. In an essay on "Apparent Anachronisms" appended to *Caesar and Cleopatra* [2] Shaw explained his position in a way which seems a close parallel to Golding's view of historical distance:

The only way to write a play which shall convey to the general public an impression of antiquity is to make the characters speak blank verse and abstain from reference to steam, telegraphy, or any of the material conditions of their existence. The more ignorant men are, the more convinced are they that their little parish and

[1] "Before the Beginning," a review of *World Prehistory*, by Grahame Clark, *The Spectator*, May 26, 1961, p. 768.
[2] First published in 1901. The present text is taken from the Penguin edition of *Caesar and Cleopatra* (London and Baltimore, 1951), pp. 128–29.

their little chapel is an apex to which civilization and philosophy has painfully struggled up the pyramid of time from a desert of savagery. Savagery, they think, became barbarism; barbarism became ancient civilization; ancient civilization became Pauline Christianity; Pauline Christianity became Roman Catholicism; Roman Catholicism became the Dark Ages; and the Dark Ages were finally enlightened by the Protestant instincts of the English race. The whole process is summed up as Progress with a capital P. And any elderly gentleman of Progressive temperament will testify that the improvement since he was a boy is enormous.

Now if we count the generations of Progressive elderly gentlemen since, say, Plato, and add together the successive improvements to which each of them has testified, it will strike us at once as an unaccountable fact that the world, instead of having been improved in 67 generations out of all recognition, presents, on the whole, a rather less dignified appearance in Ibsen's Enemy of the People than in Plato's Republic. And in truth, the period of time covered by history is far too short to allow of any perceptible progress in the popular sense of Evolution of the Human Species. The notion that there has been any such Progress since Caesar's time (less than 20 centuries) is too absurd for discussion. All the savagery, barbarism, dark ages and the rest of it of which we have any record as existing in the past, exists at the present moment. . . .

Progress, Shaw went on, is generally measured by the increasing sophistication of our methods and weapons of murder, and man's increasing command over Nature—as if "increased command over Nature included any increased command over himself (the only sort of command relevant to his evolution into a higher being). . . ."

It would be difficult for an English playwright in the twentieth century—especially one planning a play on the order of Golding's Brass Butterfly—to have escaped the pervasive

Shavian influences, particularly that of the satires based in antiquity. And whether or not Golding has ever read Shaw's easily available notes to *Caesar and Cleopatra*, it is apparent that the views of the men are, in some significant respects, strikingly similar. Even the worldly-wise Emperor is in the Shavian tradition of Plato-inspired philosopher-kings, wiser than he first appears to be, more sensitive than he first seems. In this Shavian-style high comedy of ideas, it is again the philosopher-king who seems the spokesman for the playwright's personal point of view. "The law of change is the law of God," Shaw once said (in the Preface to *Saint Joan*, 1924). So, too, Golding's Emperor understands. "You are a force of nature, Phanocles," he confesses. "There is no stopping you. I can only divert you. . . ." Leaving the world alone is no more possible than its effective guidance by reason alone. And we are left, as in *Androcles*, with the God-guided intuition of a young girl, and the mystery and glory and beauty of a world in which, paradoxically, man's inmost nature is often untrustworthy and dark.

8

CONCLUSION:

WHICH WAY THE WAVE?

ANY ESTIMATION of Golding's literary worth at this time must be tentative and blurred. Golding himself may have much more to say, biographically and literarily, before a conclusive analysis can be attempted. All that can be done now is a critical progress report, based primarily on what Golding has produced—five published novels, a novella made into a play, and a cluster of fugitive reviews and articles.

One of these last, an essay entitled "On the Crest of the Wave," proves to be vital. It acts as something of a blueprint to the Golding craft. What first strikes the eye in this essay is Golding's characteristic prose, consisting mainly of Anglo-Saxon monosyllables that are combined into crisp, angular,

sometimes balanced sentences, which achieve grace and pre-
ciseness at the same time:

I examine the *History of Herodotus*, specially translated for that
library ["Hundred Best Books"]. It has slabs of small, grey print,
less readable than Rawlinson, less faithful than Bohn. The liveliest,
easiest and most entertaining of histories has become a chore, a
duty that only a passionate determination to be educated could
stay with to the end. Yet I remember hearing of one man who read
the whole library, book by book. He was a miner and a lay reader.
What time he spent on the surface was devoted to the Lord's work.
Yet he knew there was another sphere, apart from coal and the
Lord, a sphere we might call the humanities, or culture, or education.

This is expository prose of course, and by no means the best
passage in the essay. So there are some differences between it
and what is to be found in the dramatic sections or the poetic
visions of Golding's fiction. But it still has enough of the basic
structure to act as an example, especially since it leads to several
other characteristic features deserving full attention. To begin
with, the figure of the lay miner is revealing, working as he
does at several levels and within the three spheres of humanistic
activity. Like Golding's fictional characters, he assumes not
only realistic proportions (being in actuality an ancestor of the
writer's) but also allegorical weight. Each morning, with a
bellows rigged to his foot, he blows up the fire and reads another paragraph out of "The Hundred Best Books." He stands,
or sits actually, as some Lincolnesque figure of durable self-
enlightenment.

As this picture of homely education gives way to a more
formal one, still another familiar Golding tactic becomes apparent. Peculiarly enough, in language reminiscent of Lok,

H. G. Wells is once more summoned up for rebuttal, but in a more sympathetic manner than he was in *The Inheritors:* I remember a picture," Golding writes, "a picture that is relevant. H. G. Wells describes it somewhere.[1] Two radiantly beautiful children, magnificent specimens both, are looking into the dawn. One of those hygienic and comely women who haunted Wells's imagination is kneeling by them, her arm round their shoulders, and she is pointing into the light. She is Education."

We hardly need be told what comes next. Golding is going to correct that picture, the too-hopeful and optimistic picture set forth by the rationalistic school of "Natural Philosophy." Having long worked under the pointing finger of Education, he knows the children. They are all that Wells expected, at least physically. But what of the woman? According to Golding, "She still wears the near-classical robes. . . . But her face

[1] Golding recalled the image vividly, if not the exact source. It was the first chapter of Wells's novel *The History of Mr. Polly* (1910): "I remember seeing a picture of Education—in some place. I think it was Education, but quite conceivably it represented the Empire teaching her Sons, and I have a strong impression that it was a wall-painting upon some public building in Manchester or Glasgow, but very possibly I am mistaken about that. It represented a glorious woman, with a wise and fearless face, stooping over her children, and pointing them to far horizons. The sky displayed the pearly warmth of a summer dawn, and all the painting was marvellously bright as if with the youth and hope of the delicately beautiful children in the foreground. She was telling them, one felt, of the great prospect of life that opened before them, of the splendours of sea and mountain they might travel and see, the joys of skill they might acquire, of effort and the pride of effort, and the devotions and nobilities it was theirs to achieve. Perhaps even she whispered of the warm triumphant mystery of love that comes at last to those who have patience and unblemished hearts. . . . She was reminding them of their great heritage as English children, rulers of more than one-fifth of mankind, of the obligation to do and be the best that such a pride of empire entails, of their essential nobility and knighthood, and of the restraints and charities and disciplined strength that is becoming in knights and rulers. . . ." It is possible to view almost the entire Golding *oeuvre* as an implicit response to this Wellsian image.

is fretted with the lines of worry and exasperation." The reason for her distraught appearance is apparent. Though she still points toward the light, "the little girl is yawning; and the boy is looking at his feet." What Education has had to learn is that she is being ignored, at best, and prostituted, at worst: "Education still points to the glorious dawn, officially at any rate, but has been brought to see, in a down-to-earth manner, that what we really want is technicians and civil servants."

Fortunately, the essay does not turn into still another attack on H. G. Wells. Golding willingly admits that education should be as Wells describes it, that Wells at least had some plan of "Natural Philosophy." Society has turned the plan down, because, as Golding puts it, "The overtones were too vast, too remote, too useless on the national scale, too emphatically on the side of 'knowing' rather than 'doing.' " Instead it may be a hidden C. P. Snow picture of education and society that Golding is really trying to correct. "On the Crest of the Wave" can be read as a reaction to *The Two Cultures*. Golding's point of correction (one that Snow was not entirely unaware of himself) is that there are three "cultures" abroad today, not two—that of the humanities, that of pure science (or Natural Philosophy), and that of technology. It is this last "culture" which threatens to envelop everything and everybody. For Golding, technocracy—the dehumanizing power of things—constitutes the modern evil. Under the sway of this hard and brassy butterfly (see *The Brass Butterfly*), education has given way to training; value judgments, to measurement. All of this, Golding insists, is extremely regrettable: "Our humanity rests in the capacity to make value judgments, unscientific assessments, the power to decide that this is right, that wrong, this ugly, that beautiful, this just, that unjust. Yet these are precisely the questions which 'Science' is not qualified to answer with its measurement and analysis." Trying to make it clear, with the aid of quotation marks, that he is not attacking science as such, Golding nevertheless understands the dangers involved even in an attack upon technology and its offspring. He knows the result may be critical damnation and general unpopularity; and in this respect, he may indeed have been thinking of what Martin Green had written about him just a month before the appearance of "Crest of the Wave": "Golding is perhaps the most extreme example of that sullen distaste for the contemporary which Snow describes as cankering modern literary intellectuals and as deriving from their rejection of science."

No one who has read a novel of Golding's doubts that he is rejecting something. But it seems to be man's inhuman use of science rather than science itself. The (again typical) irony of his title "On the Crest of the Wave" underscores that rejection. We may be on the crest of a wave—but what kind of crest and what kind of wave? Where is all this universal education, or materialistic training, rather, leading to? Rueful Education still points toward the true and the good and the beautiful, but she seems to be riding captive in another direction—"to the world where it is better to be envied than ignored, better to be well paid than happy, better to be successful than good, better to be vile, than vile-esteemed."

Whether Golding simply has a "sullen distaste for the contemporary" which stems from a "rejection of science" has to be decided by every reader for himself. Golding, however, does something to explain his own cast of mind when he writes, near the beginning of this essay: "I am by nature an optimist; but a defective logic—or a logic which I sometimes hope desperately is defective makes a pessimist of me." And without necessarily intending to do so, by announcing the plan of the essay, he informs us of the manner in which he has habitually worked out his fiction: "Perhaps the best thing to do is put forward the depressing logic first, with all its grey implications; and conclude with a happier irrational section, which will roundly contradict the first part." Given certain technical variations, this statement accounts for the process by which he has worked out all of his novels with the exception of *Pincher Martin*, which remains grayly and even blackly pessimistic throughout. In *Lord of the Flies* at least a specious light appears in the form of the whitely attired naval officer (even though Simon is the true possessor of the light, not Piggy or this naval officer); and, of course, the ending of the novel does roundly, if ironically, "contradict the first part." At the conclusion of *The Inheritors* (in a subtle and artistically sound way) Tuami is shown searching for a point of light to use against the darkness. At the end of *Free Fall* Sammy Mountjoy, crying out for help, bursts from the darkness of his prison cell, experiencing a "flake of fire . . . miraculous and pentecostal." And in *The Spire* Dean Jocelin reaches mystical enlightenment in the revelation of an apple tree just before the words "God! God! God!" flutter from his dying lips.

Almost fervently Golding tries to salvage the light of optimism from the darkness of logical pessimism. Each time he does so through the agency of human worth, of creative genius. Thus Simon, Tuami, Sammy, and Jocelin are all presented as seers, vision-makers, or creators. They are true descendants of the old miner and his bellows. "The only education," Golding roundly declares, "is self-education, and the human spirit, at its best, is self-propelled. Man is a single species in the physically identifiable sense, but Beethoven and I are as different as a tiger and a rabbit. The human spirit is wider and more complex than the whole of the physical evolutionary system. . . ." This sounds both mystical and messianic, for whatever desperate hope he has Golding puts in mankind's ability to produce Beethovens, Shakespeares, and St. Augustines. But (and this may be the real weakness in his work) he has never been able to expand upon this mystic faith in his fiction. A glimmer of hope comes and goes—never any real show of human warmth and love *and* ascendant ability at the same time. Indicatively enough, the Augustine he admires is not that of *The City of God*, but of the *Confessions*—"wherein the spirit of European man for better or worse, was re-experienced, suffered, and remade." This is the suffering and confessing Augustine, if not the "remade," who is the spiritual father of *Pincher Martin*, *The Spire*, and, particularly, *Free Fall*. Each of these works is fully confessional in tone and import, although only the last mentioned is done as a *récit* in the first person singular. And all show Augustinian agonies of the flesh in conjunction with the acceptance or rejection of contrition and grace.

Golding has admitted to having tried in his own way for over twenty years to write what he would define as significant literature. "On the Crest of the Wave" is a tangential examination of the times in which he has made the attempt, and the kind of audience that might be available for it. These are times in which Golding seems modestly aware of his own mission as a modern-day Augustine of minor order. His novels preach against the sins of the flesh in fleshly colors—sins so strong to his nostrils that there is often a cloacal stench hovering around his most revealing scenes. In the foulness and darkness, through glints of light transmitted by his own artistic power, he searches for the spirit of man in a new and fearsome age.

To some people it comes as a matter of some relief that a

twentieth-century author has once again—in a manner more austere than Graham Greene's—taken to writing extremely viable materials that deal with God, Original Sin, Confession, the Holy Ghost, and Pentecostal flakes. Even in the popular imagination God cannot be made lively by way of bingo or mass meetings in Madison Square Garden. As a soul-searching Augustinian of sorts, Golding seems to have a better chance of bringing the word to certain quarters. With him there is some chance of affecting minds otherwise unapproachable. In fact, Golding's ability to make nonbelievers and disbelievers pause over many of the old questions they thought had been packed away for good may very well be one of his strongest bids for permanence. He has been able to make fiction awaken conscience.

Certainly it is this programmatic aspect of his work—this role of the lay preacher—that has led to such articles as Sam Hynes's "Novels of a Religious Man," which is perhaps the most sensible treatment of the matter. It is likewise this aspect which draws the admiration, or at least critical attention, of the *Christian Science Monitor* and Roman Catholic journals like *The Critic* and *America*, where heady theological discussions have resulted. And it is this same homiletic quality which earns Golding the admiration of critics like Edmund Fuller, who has always favored writers of a strong moral nature, in the most conventional sense of that outmoded phrase.

Assuredly Golding deserves to be looked at from the religious point of view. One of his growing number of extrafictional pronouncements—this included in a letter to John Peter—is enough to assure us that the preacher in him is active: "The cellar in *Pincher Martin* represents more than childhood terrors; a whole philosophy in fact—suggesting that God is the thing we turn away from into life, and therefore we hate and fear him and make a darkness there." But luckily for us all Golding's works are also the novels of a literary man, and those of a man with an exceedingly tough grasp of what it is like to live with the crusty detail of this earth's surface. Golding the artist and Golding the man are often in conflict with the preacher—just as Golding the onetime science student is in conflict with the antiscientist; and Golding the optimist is in conflict with Golding the pessimist. William Faulkner said that the only kind of literature worth writing is that in which the human heart is in conflict with itself. And in this Golding seems to qualify—especially if we take heart to mean mind and spirit. That is why, even after Golding has told us the moral he intended with a book like *Pincher Martin*—in which the "hero" is condemned to eternal suffering—we can still find the heroic quality of Pincher and read the book with sympathy for his courage and intelligence and gallant attempt to fly in the face of the universe. Golding has built better than he claims and perhaps better than he intended, because of his manhood, because of his art. The preacher might have us see only a false Prometheus (P—M—?), one whose egocentrism is the deadliest of sins—oh, Prideful Martin! His God hounds him, tasks him, tortures him in a purgatory that does not purge. But the artist gives us a Martin who refuses to let go, refuses to give up the only thing he knows—himself as a man. To a certain extent, it is the theme of Ahab once again, brought to bear this time not on a whale but on a molar.

Eventually it is the art of Golding we must deal with and not his morals. Only in a special sense can criticism be interested in how these novels create a scheme of religious and moral concepts—to the extent they provide a core, a viewpoint, and a tone. By themselves such concepts do not give rise to art; they must be mixed with earth and water. This is what Golding himself says thematically in *The Spire*, as he beautifully depicts the reversible paradox involved in the holiness of secular art and the secularization of holy art.

To reach some kind of final judgment, criticism, in the form of analysis, can tell us something about the craft of William Golding: (1) that he works through strong reaction, subtly re-employing the works of others, assimilating their materials so well as to show hardly any marks of influence; (2) that he uses strong visual powers which lead to a technique heavily dependent upon description, involving full coloration and minutely sensuous depiction; (3) that he often reveals a revulsion toward the body and its functions (there is, by the way, a strange absence of normal sex in his books), with a resultant trail of cloacal images that stretch from the leavings of the young 'uns in his first novel to the messy foundations of Jocelin's spire in the last; (4) that he seeks a "meta-language," which is not to be confused with poetic effects as such, but which can so juxtapose emotion and situation as to make certain moments in life and literature luminous; and (5) that he tries to accomplish his task with an impeccable prose, something that might parallel for our time the original language of *The Odyssey*, something—in Golding's own words—at once "oral and formal," something fine enough to magnify individual blades of grass, something powerful enough to capture the "surge and thunder" of the universe.

The final critical question about Golding is simple, if the answer is not. What contribution has he made to fiction of the twentieth century and how worthwhile is that contribution? To answer we must first agree that Golding does not write novels in the usual sense of the term. He is doing something different from anybody else writing serious fiction today. He has bridged a gap between the allegory of the past and the realistic fiction of the present—moving on a line from, say, *Everyman* to *Pilgrim's Progress* to *The Scarlet Letter* to his own work. Some critics call what he is doing "parables" or "fables," and Golding himself would like to be considered the shaper, or reshaper, of "myths." His own designation comes close to the target. But perhaps it is best to think of him as a "visionist" and a "visualist" whose imagination probes out in various directions and brings to life, in a naturalistic manner, the oldest questions of human life.

How well he does this leads inevitably to the old critical concepts of originality and imagination. And as fate would have it, the answer to Golding's worth seems to be wedged between two extreme opinions, where we must, so to speak, choose between two Greens. Martin Green, in his already mentioned "Distaste for the Contemporary," sums up for the opposition by declaring that "Golding is *not importantly original* in thought or feeling," because his handling of ideas is "too predictable and too exaggerated." Peter Green, in "The World of William Golding," sums up for Golding adherents by declaring: "Despite all his self-imposed limitations, he remains *the most powerful writer, the most original, the most profoundly imaginative*, to have turned his hand to fiction in this country since the war; and if he never wrote another word his place in English letters would be secure." (Both of these opinions were delivered before the appearance of *The Spire*, but it is doubtful that that book would have done anything but reinforce each stand.)

In its own way this study should have shed some light on the question of imagination and originality. Certainly Golding's method of borrowed settings, plots, and motifs from other writers, Ballantyne, Wells, Conrad, Camus, and Ibsen, does not lead to abstract originality and wild imagination.

Certainly he does not follow what the American Neo-Humanists called the "demon of the absolute," with its one horn pointing toward Naturalism and the other to some Romantic concept of originality. (It was Rousseau who epitomized the double fault, but especially the Romantic, when he confessed that even if he were not better than other men, at least he was different.)

Golding's originality is of another order and lies in a combination of things. The conflicting tendencies of his mind (which we have noted) contribute to it in the dramatic tautness of his rendering. So does his ability to deal with transcendent questions in a mirror-clear style of pointillistic detail (an ability shared with such Americans as Emerson, Thoreau, and Frost). But it is his visual power—his earthy ability to see man's fall and Satan's rise, all in one glance at a pig's arse—that most contributes to his originality. This power, demonstrated in *Lord of the Flies*, springs from the earth and indicates that Golding is not a lily-white, Sunday-school writer. He knows many disagreeable things—things which he keeps trying to shed like old and rotten flesh (thereby producing works like *Free Fall* and *The Spire*). As the following passage demonstrates, he works on the dung-heap-and-rose principle of beauty, where the beautiful and the disgusting are mixed in typical Goldingesque manner, producing in turn their own kind of literary beauty: "More dust came down from the square shaft over the crossways. It lay here and there in modest drifts and dunes. Sun shafts were bright with it, monuments held it in little films and screes. The crusaders who lay in heraldic silence on slabs between the pillars of the nave were no longer flamboyant with heraldry, but wore filthy chain mail, or dung-coloured plate armour. . . ."

What Golding may produce in the next ten or fifteen years

is impossible to say. But he has already demonstrated—in a series of novels indicating tighter and tighter command of form and style—the ability to touch a nerve alive to the possibilities of our twentieth-century dilemma. Through his works we see that man has come this far, slipping and falling as he goes. And now—what? Does he fall once more, and this time for good? Like most of us, Golding is a bit punch-drunk from the effects of Belsen and Hiroshima. Without mentioning them in his fiction, he seems nevertheless to take us into a world of teetering brinkmanship. In his novels we pause at the depths of childhood's depravity; we peer down into the deep, free-fall well of birth and rebirth; we teeter at the top of a spire, with the last nail in hand; and we are once more placed in the presence of something truly awful—the gap between man and God—hearing with Pincher Martin what the thunder and the lightning said.

It is probably in this ability to lead us to the brink of things that Golding's basic power and originality reside. He has the glance of a fire-watcher at night, hypnotized and hypnotizing. Through his eyes we look deep into the past, and with his light we sense the drama of man's desire to create some kind of tool that can be used against the darkness, against the universal fear that we seem to be leaving as a horrible inheritance to our children. If he proves to be as humanly responsive in his vision as he has been artistically inspired, a great novelist may yet emerge from our era. Golding, unlike "Education," may be pointing toward a true dawn and moving toward it on the crest of his own wave.

BIBLIOGRAPHY

THERE ARE FEW STUDIES of Golding's work, other than book reviews, which deal exclusively with any other novel than *Lord of the Flies*. Major review articles and other publications of significance to a study of Golding have been referred to in notes and text. (They include many of Golding's own fugitive pieces.) The closest approximation to a book-length study of Golding published through 1964 is *William Golding*, a pamphlet by Samuel Hynes (1964), in the Columbia University series "Essays on Modern Writers."

Golding's novels are currently published by Harcourt, Brace & World, Inc. in the United States, and Faber and Faber Ltd in Great Britain. His first novels to be released in the U.S., however, were offered by other publishers, as the list below indicates. We have used both American and English editions in preparing this study, but have quoted from the American editions.

Major Publications by William Golding

POEMS
London & Toronto: The Macmillan Company, 1934
New York: The Macmillan Company, 1935

LORD OF THE FLIES
London: Faber & Faber, 1954
New York: Coward-McCann, 1955
New York: G. P. Putnam's Sons, 1959 (pa.)
Harmondsworth, Middlesex: Penguin Books, 1960
New York: Coward-McCann, 1962
London: Faber & Faber, 1962 (pa.)
London: Faber & Faber, 1963
New York: Odyssey Press, 1963 (pa.)

THE INHERITORS
London: Faber & Faber, 1955
London: Faber & Faber, 1961
New York: Harcourt, Brace & World, 1962
New York: Harcourt, Brace & World, 1963 (pa.)

PINCHER MARTIN
London: Faber & Faber, 1956
New York: G. P. Putnam's Sons, 1962 (pa.)
London: Penguin, 1962
London: Faber & Faber, 1962
New York: Harcourt, Brace & World, 1957 (published as *The Two Deaths of Christopher Martin*)

SOMETIME, NEVER (includes *Envoy Extraordinary*): *Three Tales of Imagination by William Golding, John Wyndham, and Mervyn Peake*
London: Eyre & Spottiswoode, 1956
New York: Ballantine, 1962 (pa.)

BRASS BUTTERFLY (play)
London: Faber & Faber, 1958
New York: New American Library, 1962 (in *The Genius of the Later English Theater*) (pa.)

FREE FALL
London: Faber & Faber, 1959
New York: Harcourt, Brace & World, 1960
London: Faber & Faber, 1961 (pa.)
New York: Harcourt, Brace & World, 1962 (pa.)

THE SPIRE
London: Faber & Faber, 1964
New York: Harcourt, Brace & World, 1964

Contributions to Periodicals by William Golding

ALMOST ALL OF Golding's contributions to periodicals represent his career as book reviewer for *The Spectator* from 1960 through 1962; however, many of his *Spectator* pieces, including reviews, are partly (or entirely) autobiographical or personal, including those cited in various places in this book, as well as all the entries in the latter half of 1961 and the three in 1962.

"In Retreat," *The Spectator*, 204 (March 25, 1960), 448–49
"Raider," *The Spectator*, 204 (May 20, 1960), 741
"Islands," *The Spectator*, 204 (June 10, 1960), 844–46
"On the Crest of the Wave," *The Times Literary Supplement*, June 17, 1960, p. 387. Reprinted in *The Writer's Dilemma* (London: Oxford University Press, 1961), pp. 42–51

"Headmasters," *The Spectator*, 205 (August 12, 1960), 252

"In My Ark," *The Spectator*, 205 (September 16, 1960), 409

"Man of God," *The Spectator*, 205 (October 7, 1960), 530

"Billy the Kid," *The Spectator*, 205 (November 25, 1960), 808, 811

"Prospect of Eton," *The Spectator*, 205 (November 25, 1960), 856–57

"Thin Partitions," *The Spectator*, 206 (January 13, 1961), 49

"The Rise of Love," *The Spectator*, 206 (February 10, 1961), 194

"Androids All," *The Spectator*, 206 (February 24, 1961), 263

"All or Nothing," *The Spectator*, 206 (March 24, 1961), 410

"Before the Beginning," *The Spectator*, 206 (May 26, 1961), 768

"Astronaut by Gaslight," *The Spectator*, 206 (June 9, 1961), 841–42

"It's a Long Way to Oxyrhynchus," *The Spectator*, 207 (July 7, 1961), 9

"Tolstoy's Mountain," *The Spectator*, 207 (September 8, 1961), 325–26

"A Touch of Insomnia," *The Spectator*, 207 (October 27, 1961), 569, 571

"The Glass Door," *The Spectator*, 207 (November 24, 1961), 732–33

"Body and Soul," *The Spectator*, 208 (January 19, 1962), 65–66

"Gradus ad Parnassum," *The Spectator*, 209 (September 7, 1962), 327, 329

"Surge and Thunder," *The Spectator*, 209 (September 14, 1962), 370